The Pen
Commandments

STEVEN FRANK

The Pen Commandments

Steven Frank has been an English teacher for more than ten years. He lives in Los Angeles with his wife and children.

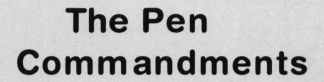

The Pen Commandments

A Guide for the Beginning Writer

STEVEN FRANK

Anchor Books

A Division of Random House, Inc. | *New York*

Thou shalt take pleasure in Thy pen

FIRST ANCHOR BOOKS EDITION, SEPTEMBER 2004

Copyright © 2003 by Steven Frank

Grateful acknowledgment is made to Alfred A. Knopf for permission
to reprint the poem "Dreams" from *The Collected Poems of Langston Hughes*
by Langston Hughes. Copyright © 1994 by The Estate of
Langston Hughes. Reprinted by permission of Alfred A. Knopf,
a division of Random House, Inc.

The Library of Congress has cataloged the Pantheon edition as follows:
Frank, Steven, 1963–
The pen commandments : a guide for the beginning writer / Steven Frank.
p.   cm.
Includes bibliographical references.
1. English language—Rhetoric.
2. English language—Composition and exercises. I. Title.
PE1408.F57 2003
808'.042—dc21
2003040450

Anchor ISBN: 1-4000-3229-6

Book design by Johanna S. Roebas

www.anchorbooks.com

Printed in the United States of America
10 9 8 7 6 5 4 3 2

For Sophie, who brought me inspiration,
For Sammy, who brought me luck,
And for Julie, who brought me Sophie and Sam

When I was seven, I said to my mother, may I close my door? And she said, yes, but why do you want to close your door? And I said because I want to think. And when I was eleven, I said to my mother, may I lock my door? And she said, yes, but why do you want to lock your door? And I said because I want to write.

—DOROTHY WEST

Contents

Preface

There are certain books, usually with pictures, that kids sneak off their parents' shelf and take a naughty look at. Here is a book that parents will be sneaking off their kids' shelf. It doesn't have any pictures, but it is full of words—words about words and language and writing.

On my first day as an English teacher ten years ago, I entered a classroom completely unprepared. I hadn't been to graduate school. I knew nothing about classroom management, lesson planning, or cognitive theory. I had been hired on a hunch the Friday before, and this was the first Monday of a new career.

On *your* first day of school, all you have to do is show up. But your teacher is supposed to come with an arsenal of assignments, a head bursting with ideas, a bag full of tricks to capture your attention and stimulate your mind. On my first day the bag was more or less empty, so I decided to play Hangman with the students and let them choose their own methods of execution. It was an offbeat way to begin the year, but everybody perked right up, and together we had our first lesson about English: it's supposed to be fun. The words I used came from the myth of Orpheus, which I read aloud to the class. We then put Hades on trial for being so cruel to mythology's greatest musician. The jury of twelve sentenced the Captain of Hell to an eternity of cleaning up after his three-headed dog. There was a spirit of adventure in the room, and just before the bell rang, I gave my first writing assignment: a fantasy piece about what you *didn't do* over summer vacation.

The essays I received were full of mistakes in spelling, grammar, and punctuation. But they were just as amply filled with imagination, humor, and originality. Although I had none of the official credentials for being an English teacher, I discovered I had the most important ones: a respect for children and a love of language, which I shared with my young charges.

Over time, and with experience teaching students from nine to nineteen years old, I realized that it wasn't enough just to play with words; we had to master them along the way. With the help of a new teacher's best friend—trial and error—I developed a method for teaching people how to write. Ten years later here is the result. I hope *The Pen Commandments* is a useful guide and a playful one too. If you should happen to catch your parents sneaking a peek at this book, don't embarrass them by saying, "What do you think you're doing?" Instead, back quietly out of your own room and let them have their fun. After all, when they were growing up, they had to get this information from boring textbooks or tyrannical teachers who could spank them if they forgot a topic sentence. So go easy on them. Leave a copy lying around. Maybe, in return, they'll leave one of their books lying around for you.

Introduction

You're probably wondering if you have to read the introduction. Introductions can be very long; I promise you a short one. They can give away important information that the book itself reveals; I won't divulge any secrets here. But I will tell you what a good introduction does, and then you can decide whether to read it or to skip ahead to Chapter 1.

A good introduction, like a good party host, welcomes the reader at the front door. It offers you a hand and makes you feel at home. And the way it makes you feel at home is by letting you know what to expect once you step inside.

The Pen Commandments will teach you how to write. It isn't a textbook with exercises for homework; you already have one of those taking up too much space in your backpack. It isn't a book on grammar, although you'll find some advice on grammar as it relates to good writing, and you can look in the appendix for the Top Ten Grammar Mistakes You Shouldn't Make. It isn't a book on poetry or fiction; these are subjects I love so much, I think they deserve books of their own.

But the basic principles of writing, the ones you need to write your way to success in school and out of it, the ones that will energize, inspire, and preserve you—these are waiting on the other side of the door.

So come on in. The only pass you need is a pen.

The Pen
Commandments

One

Thou Shalt
Honor Thy Reader

ON THE FIRST DAY OF SCHOOL where I teach, the students all line up in the yard according to grade. They mill about, getting reacquainted after a summer apart, and they tell stories. One year I heard someone cry out, "Ewwww, that's disgusting!" I turned and saw a small crowd huddled around a boy named Jason who was describing the oral surgery he had had back in June.

"They found out I had an extra tooth growing down from the roof of my mouth. If we did nothing, it would keep on growing till it touched my tongue. So the dentist said he'd have to pull it."

"Did it hurt?" asked one girl.

"Well, when he cut the hole around the tooth, that wasn't so bad. But then he took a pair of pliers and started twisting it back and forth, like a nail. That I felt."

"Was there a lot of blood?" a boy asked.

"That depends on how you define *a lot*. Let's just say I couldn't spit fast enough and kept swallowing instead. Finally he got the tooth out, jammed some cotton up there, and told me to hold it in place with my tongue."

"What's it look like now?"

Jason smiled a thin, wicked smile. Then he threw back his head and opened wide for all the kids to gaze at—and be grossed out by—the crater in the roof of his mouth. There was a roar of disgusted cries, and then one kid said, "Can I see that again?"

That's when it hit me: a writing assignment designed to gross us out, to keep us gathered around a composition the way the kids had all gathered around Jason. The topic: "An Accident That Happened." The goal: include so many gory details that at least five of your classmates will either hurl their lunch or skip their dinner. Now you may ask how a writer who incites mass vomiting is respecting his reader, but I invite you to visit my classroom on the day these compositions are read aloud. People love to hear the stories behind scars just as much as they love to tell them.

The Right Topic

The leading cause of writer apathy among today's students is bad topics. "Write about your summer vacation." "Describe your room." "Describe your family." "Write a letter to the editor." "Write a plot summary." "Write a character analysis." "Write a report about the uses of zinc oxide in a developed society." Write a this, write a that, write a write a write—why write at all?

If you're not inspired by a writing topic, ask to change it.

Ask your teacher if you can describe your family from the dog's point of view, or the fish's. Ask if your plot summary can include blanks so that your classmates can try to guess the title when you read it aloud. Ask if your character analysis can include a literary personals ad to help your character find a date. Don't ask—*send* your letter to a real editor of a real newspaper. Or better yet, start a newspaper of your own. Sell subscriptions to pay for the Xeroxing costs. Do whatever you can to feel passionate about writing, because if you find the topic boring to write, your reader will find it just as boring to read.

When my brother-in-law Steve was a freshman in college, he had to write an essay entitled "A World Without Books." The professor had the poor judgment to announce the assignment in mid-March, just as the NCAA basketball tournament was getting under way. Steve was too busy placing bets to ponder a world without books, so he ignored the topic until the night before it was due. At eleven P.M., after UCLA had trounced Michigan and won Steve enough money for a weekend in Tahoe, he sat down to his Smith-Corona typewriter and wrote a perfectly suitable topic sentence: "A world without books would be a miserable place in which to live." Within seconds Steve's head fell forward and crashed onto the keys of his typewriter. Three hours later he woke up, squinted at his paper, and saw the topic sentence followed by a row of zzzzzzzzzzzzzzzzzzzzzzzz's.

Two cups of coffee and four No-Doz tablets later, Steve tried again. To warm up his typing fingers, he retyped the topic sentence: "A world without books would be a miserable place in which to live." The third cup of coffee was still steaming when his head lolled forward and thudded to the typewriter. At six o'clock the next morning, there was the same topic sentence, this time followed by a row of *ppppppppppppppppppppppppp*'s.

With *z*'s and *p*'s imprinted on his forehead and not much more on the page, and with the essay due in less than three hours, Steve got the sillies. He began to type over and over: "A WORLD WITHOUT BOOKS. A WORLD WITHOUT BOOKS. A WORLD WITHOUT BOOKS . . ." Near the bottom of the page he accidentally typed something different: A WORLD WITHOUT BOOKS. A WORLD WITHOUT BOOKS. A WORLD WITHOUT BOOKIES. He stopped and reread that phrase: A WORLD WITHOUT BOOKIES. "That's it!" he thought. "That's something I can write about."

He loaded a fresh sheet. "A world without bookies would be a miserable place in which to live," he began. And for the next hour and a half Steve wrote a college essay on a topic that thrilled him.

Do you know what his grade was?

A-plus. The professor was blown away by the originality and irreverence of his essay. Not only did he reward him with the highest grade in the class, he thanked him by reading the composition out loud to a lecture hall crammed with five hundred students. "Of the all the essays I read, this was the only one I enjoyed."

Your first reader is often a teacher. Honor thy reader: we're desperate to be entertained.

Show, Don't Tell

Once you've found a topic that keeps you awake, you can honor thy reader by keeping him awake too. While you can't control the flow of caffeine into your reader's blood, you can control the flow of words into his brain. Don't use too many, but be vivid with the ones you choose: show, don't tell.

Early in the school year I ask my students to write an outrageous excuse for why their homework wasn't done. If the excuse is convincing, I let them use it like a get-out-of-jail-free card instead of turning in one assignment during the semester.

One student who did not respect her reader dashed off the cliché, "My dog ate it." "My dog ate it" is as old as a bloodhound who's lost his sense of smell, but even it can be delivered with a little more panache. A more entertaining excuse might have gone, "My homework lay on the floor in slimy, torn pieces. There were teeth marks in the margins and paw prints on my opening paragraph. I followed the trail of slobber into the kitchen, where my dog sat with my conclusion in his mouth." That brief paragraph *shows*, through storytelling, what the first sentence merely *tells*, in flat uninteresting fact. It's more fun to read because it hooks you with an image—the slimy, torn pieces on the floor—and then leads you to another image—the dog with a conclusion in his mouth—to explain it. You, the reader, get to complete the puzzle. You aren't passively receiving information; you have to work for it, and the result is a sense of accomplishment and fun. (By the way, the rewritten version is the work of the student who wrote the dog excuse in the first place. With a little help from her classmates, she was able to improve her writing a thousand percent.)

You can always write, "Last night it rained." But isn't it more intriguing to show us that it rained by creating a picture or a sound for the morning after? "I was awakened by the sound of tires splashing through puddles of water. Pulling back the curtain, I saw that the sun had sliced through the clouds and was busy mopping up the streets."

Is this a violation of Pen Commandment 2, Thou Shalt Not Waste Words? It's true I'm using more words to express what could be stated in fewer, but I'm not just adding *words* to the sentence; I'm adding an *image*. "Last night it rained" won't stay with the reader nearly as long as the idea of puddles being mopped up by the sun. Less is sometimes less, and more is sometimes more.

Feed Your Reader Well

You can also honor thy reader by not serving him a skimpy meal. Your writing needs to cast a spell on the reader, lure him into a chair and keep him there, engaged, challenged, and well fed. If, for example, you're writing a realtor's brochure for a dream house in the year 2550, it's not enough to describe it as "an awesome home with all the comforts that technology can provide." Your reader wants to know what those comforts are. Will your dream house feature a shower bed that wakes you with a gentle spray of warm water? Will it come with a virtual closet that lets you see how you'll look in an outfit before you put it on? Will it know just the right music to play for your shifting moods?

If you are writing a composition called "_____s Make the Best Pets," in which you describe the most outlandish non-domesticated animal you can imagine bringing home, try to write beyond the obvious. Sure, having a pet giraffe would force you to blow the roof off your house and plant many more trees, but how else would it change your life? Would you have to swap your sedan for a convertible? Would you make enemies at the movies every time you and your giraffe sat in the front row?

Would you become the first pick on a basketball team if you and your pet were partners? You might even have to buy a skip loader to keep the backyard tidy.

Where do these ideas come from? For some people, right off the top of the head, but for most of us, the only thing that comes off the top of the head is dandruff. Ideas worthy of your reader come from someplace deeper and more satisfying to scratch. Give yourself enough time to reach there.

One effective technique is to brainstorm before you write. A brainstorm is the initial explosion of ideas you might have on a topic:

SAMPLE BRAINSTORM

TOPIC: You are Earth's ambassador to an alien planet. What three things will you take to introduce the human race to the aliens?

You spill ideas onto a page and circle the useful ones. You then draw spokes between main ideas and their offshoots. The main ideas will become topic sentences for paragraphs; the offshoots will become supporting sentences. If I were to expand this brainstorm into an essay, I would plan for three main paragraphs: one on a ball, one on a dictionary, and a third on a McDonald's Happy Meal. My brainstorm has a number of good points I can develop within each paragraph: the ball, a sign of friendship with the aliens, can teach them about the human need for exercise and fun; the dictionary can introduce them to the English language and teach them how to pronounce and spell words; and the McDonald's Happy Meal will help them

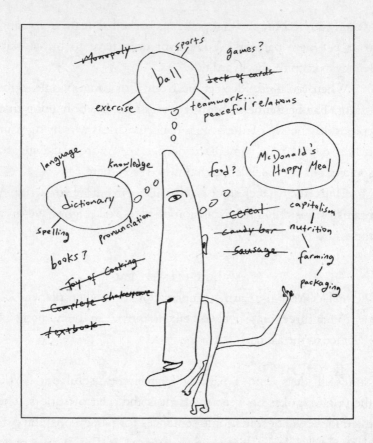

understand our physiology, our economics, and our taste in food.

On days when compositions are read aloud, I forbid the class to talk while a student reads. As soon as she finishes, however, I want the class to get noisy, either with applause, helpful criticism, or the Hunger Chant. The Hunger Chant permits the students to act like underfed orphans. When a writer hasn't given enough examples, details, or support, I urge everyone to shout,

"We want more! We want more! We want more!" The assault usually delivers the message, and the second draft is far more satisfying than the first.

When you finish a piece of writing, listen for the Hunger Chant. The best time to adjust the portions is before you serve the meal.

Avoid Giving Your Reader Whiplash

Have you ever been in a car accident? I certainly hope not, but if you have, you'll know what I mean when I say don't give your reader whiplash.

My first encounter with whiplash occurred on a Friday afternoon twenty years ago. I was driving through the intersection of Pico Boulevard and Fairfax Avenue in Los Angeles when a truck ran the red light and smashed into the right side of my car. Just then a second truck traveling in the opposite direction ran the same light and smashed into the left side of my car. I felt like a spinner in a board game, only the players were fighting over who got to spin first.

Since then I've suffered many instances of whiplash, but none of them in a car. The whiplash I've had has been confined to the classroom, where I listen to my students read their compositions:

> The most embarrassing moment of my life occurred on my tenth birthday, when my mother dropped my cake. My friends and I were shouting, "We want cake! We want cake!" when all of a sudden my mom comes out of the kitchen carrying a beautiful chocolate cake ablaze

with candles. She looks up at us and doesn't see the hot wheel track that we'd set up on the floor. The next thing I knew, my mom tripped over the tracks. The candles blew out on her way down, and she lands with her face in the center of the cake.

Did you notice the abrupt change in tense in the second sentence? Did you feel your mind being jerked back and forth between past and present? Uncomfortable, isn't it? I have often thought of hiring a personal injury attorney to sue my students for the mental whiplash that they cause whenever they change tense like this, but on a teacher's salary I can't even afford the parking at a law firm. Instead, I try to show them that by wavering between past and present, they confuse the reader and break the spell of reading itself. It's better to choose a single tense and be faithful to it.

Don't Repeat Yourself

What did you do today that you didn't do yesterday? Did you wear mismatched shoes just for the fun of it? Did you sleep with your feet at the head of the bed and your head at the foot? Most likely you began your day with breakfast as usual. I know I began mine with a twenty-minute run with my dog Lucy, a shower, a shave, and a cup of coffee from the same mug I used the day before. Most of us are creatures of habit. We live by the clock, we learn by rote, we're led by routine. It explains why we're so starved for variety, and no one wants it more than your reader.

Of all the Western languages, and possibly of all the world's languages, English gives us the most words. You could try counting them (the latest edition of the Oxford English Dictionary puts the number around 500,000, not including another half-million scientific, technical, and slang words; German has around 135,000, French fewer than 100,000), or you could take my word for it. The enormous cache of words in English means longer spelling tests, more trips to the dictionary, and more nuances to grasp. But it also means we can delight our readers with something new in every sentence. It means we never have to repeat ourselves.

Why *do* we repeat ourselves? Is it because we're lazy, dim-witted, or brain-dead? Is it because our entire vocabulary fits inside a Dixie riddle cup? Or is it because we forget which words we've used a sentence or two before? I know that most of my students are neither dull nor lazy nor neurologically impaired. If they did have infinitesimal vocabularies, they wouldn't be able to read the challenging books they devour all year long. But many of them *do* repeat themselves on the page, and they do so because they let themselves get distracted.

The best defense against a derailed train of thought is focus. And here I'll deliberately repeat myself: *focus, focus, focus!* Focus on the paragraph you are writing, not on the rerun of *Scooby-Doo* your little brother is watching in the next room. A sentence is a trail of words. Knowing what lies behind you is just as important as knowing what lies ahead.

One of my students wrote a homework excuse about a four-legged thief who ran off with his essay. "I was petting Snoops when he stole my paper and ran out of the room. I was looking for him when I heard the ripping and crunching of paper." I asked this student if he was aware he'd used the same pattern

I was . . . ing when twice in a row. He said he didn't remember using it in the first sentence, because he'd taken a cookie break before writing the second. "They were big cookies," he confessed. Big or small, fresh or stale, the cookie should be your reward for finishing the essay, not the other way around.

There are very few books I force my younger students to buy or check out from the library. One is *The Phantom Tollbooth* by Norton Juster. It is a gem of storytelling and wordplay, a joy to read as I'm sure it was to write. Another book I recommend is a thesaurus. A thesaurus is not a relative of brontosaurus or stegosaurus (although it is so infrequently consulted you'd think it was extinct too). A thesaurus is a book of words and their synonyms (*syn* = "same"; *nym* = "word"), alternatives that can surprise your reader and offer him relief from his habit-driven days. Most word processors give you a thesaurus at the stroke of a key (shift F7 on mine).

One student wrote an analysis of the horror genre. She read several scary stories and discovered that they all had certain features in common. In her essay she used the word *spooky* four times in six sentences. I drew six goblins around the four *spooky*'s: the first goblin was alert and smiling; the eyes of the second were slightly narrower; the smile of the third had faded; the fourth goblin was in a coma.

The girl got the message. On her second draft, three of the four *spooky*'s had been replaced with *eerie, macabre,* and *ghostly*. This time I drew delighted goblins around all four words.

The third book I make students buy is a dictionary. Use the dictionary to learn the meaning of words you fall in love with. *Sobriquet. Waggish. Lambent. Wangle. Elucidate. Cantankerous.*

Curmudgeon. Humuhumunukunukuapua (it's a Hawaiian fish). These can be words you overhear in conversation, words you read in a book, or words that you have to study for the SAT.

When you meet a human being you like, you ask for the person's phone number and then write it in your phone book, the Bible of your social life. Well, why not start a second phone book for all the words you meet? Instead of recording their phone numbers or e-mail addresses, record their definitions, their parts of speech, and a brief example of how they like to be used in a sentence. Just as your circle of human friends expands, your circle of vocabulary friends will expand too, and you'll be surprised how often you run into them.

Also use the dictionary to check the words you find in a thesaurus. A good dictionary will give you a definition and an example of the word in action. Make sure that the spirit of the word (its connotation) is just right for your sentence; if not, find another. *Jalopy* might be the perfect word to describe your uncle's falling-down 1980 Ford, but it could ruin the style of your grandpa's 1960 Mustang. If you used the word *thirsty* a paragraph ago and you're looking for a synonym, *parched* might apply to your throat after a long walk in the sun, but it will spoil the taste of fresh lemonade if that's what you're thirsty for. Also, pay attention to the part of speech. If you want a synonym for *secret,* you don't want to use *clandestine* when the *secret* you're looking to replace is a noun. A hiding place or affair may be *clandestine* (adjective), but you don't keep it a *clandestine* (noun) from your friends.

Your dictionary and your thesaurus are inseparable allies in your writing: they're the salt and pepper of the page.

Find Your Writer's Voice

Some writers show little respect for their reader by writing the way they talk. While reading their essays, I have an urge to call out, "Stop talking! I'm in the middle of your essay!" But when I look up, I see that I'm actually home at my desk, miles out of range of their speaking voice. And yet it's coming in loud and clear.

Here is a passage from an eighth grader's analysis of the Berenstain Bears (the assignment was to analyze a series of children's books): *A thing that all the stories have is in all the stories there's a moral and in all the stories someone learns something. Like in "Too Much Junk Food" the bears learn they've got to cut down on sweets and stuff.*

When a student can't stop talking in class, I will, for the sake of silence, tape his mouth shut. If I could find the region of the brain responsible for the chatty writing style, I would put tape around it too. But the only one who can silence the conversational voice in your head is you. After several drafts, the writer of the Berenstain Bears essay silenced hers: *One feature that all the stories have in common is that they teach a moral. In "Too Much Junk Food," for example, the bears learn that exercise is important and that eating sweets is permissible, but only in moderation.*

The best advice I can give to speakwriters is to slow down. There is a hidden world of language beneath the surface of our thoughts, and to get there you have to travel at nearly zero miles per hour. Most people don't realize that this place exists, but when they force themselves to slow down and float in the Language Lane, they find a warm current of words, like a bath. And they discover that these are not the same words they use while talking. They're not necessarily stodgy or formal or complicated words, but they are words that we choose (or that choose us) for a reason.

You should also follow the advice offered by one of my daughter's talking stuffed animals, a three-inch-high mixed-breed brown-and-white puppy. When you press his belly, he says, "Be like me; put your nose in a good book!" This wisdom is worth far more than the $3.95 we spent on the toy. It invites us to plug our ears for a moment against everyday spoken English and listen to language in its crafted, polished state. If we could silence expressions like *you know, really, awesome, totally, for sure, 'cause, a lot, like, sort of,* and *neat* for thirty minutes a day and replace them with expressions like "a pandemonium of pain" (Robert Nye), "the smell of apples turned to cider under trees" (Ray Bradbury), "the illustrious and never-to-be-sufficiently extolled cavalier, Don Quixote de la Mancha" (Cervantes), "a truth universally acknowledged that a single man in possession of a large fortune must be in want of a wife" (Jane Austen), "the tyranny of human beings" (George Orwell), "the tortures of slow starvation" (Charles Dickens), or "what fools these mortals be!" (Shakespeare), we'd begin to hear the difference between chatter and writing.

Be like that stuffed doggie—put *your* nose in a good book too. What you'll find is a dance of words to the beat of language, a demonstration of how it's done, and an inspiration to do it yourself.

Don't Leave Home Without It

But remember, most of what you write will make an appearance in the world: it will meet a reader. And just as you wouldn't leave the house for a party before making sure your hair was as spiky, as gelled, or as purple as can be, don't let your writing leave the house before it too is as polished as can be.

The first reader of everything you write should be you. Often my students stand at the front of the class to read their compositions aloud, only to blink in confusion when they stumble over a word misspelled, misused, or just plain missing. "Can you read my handwriting, Mr. Frank?" they sometimes ask. And sometimes I can. "Did I write that?" they wonder. Unless you hired a ghostwriter, yes, you did. "How do you spell *countries*? I think I wrote it wrong." Meanwhile, the class loses interest, and the student feels embarrassed or dejected. Spare yourself this awkwardness by checking your own work at least once before you turn in it and, more important, before you share it with an audience.

Of course, one set of eyes, especially your own, is never enough. I'm lucky—I married a writer. I don't let anything I write leave the house without asking my wife to read it over first. Even if you don't have a professional in the home to edit your essays, you can find a friend, a mom, a dad, a sibling, or a neighbor to look over your work before you turn it in. Honor thy reader—tuck in your commas, straighten your spelling, comb your punctuation marks. Choose words as carefully as you'd choose an outfit for the prom. And get rid of the wrinkles before you walk out the door.

Honor Thyself Too

We live in a world increasingly hostile to free time; students are assaulted by homework, parents are abducted by their jobs, and people everywhere are rushing to the next appointment, activity, or event. In fact, we're in such a hurry that our feet are making the earth spin faster—and time really is speeding up.

We've lost our solitude too. We walk around with electronic leashes clipped to our handbags, backpacks, and belts. As soon as we get a moment of silence, a moment to think, our hips vibrate or our pockets ring, and the thought is chased away. I know people who always take the stairs because they're afraid that their pagers or cell phones won't get reception in an elevator. And while this may be good for the heart, it's terrible for the soul.

There is a way to fight back—with your pen. Every sentence you write is a sign of defiance against the undertow of time. When you write, you aren't just leaking ink onto the page; you are leaving a piece of yourself permanently behind. And by writing, you carve a small space out of the frenzied, intrusive world and you say, "Hands off! Not here. This place is for me." And it's in *this* place, of silence and solitude and peace, that you are free to form your own thoughts without anybody else butting in.

When you write, no one is listening yet. It's like getting ready for a party and having all the time you need to settle on the perfect outfit, the most natural way to present yourself as you really are. Just as you might try on different styles of clothing, you can try out different styles of writing. Be silly if you want. Be imaginative and free. Take risks. Experiment. Eventually, you'll find a voice that's comfortable, that suits you, that *is* you.

Your writer's voice is your mind's fingerprint, but if you don't use it, it will fade. Keep a journal—and keep it private. Write letters, not just e-mails. Letters get saved in a shoebox or a drawer; they get discovered years and sometimes generations after they were written. E-mails get deleted, often as soon as they are read. Write poems too. Write one every time you fall in love—or out. Give one as a Christmas present instead of a tie; it will last longer and be appreciated more. Write captions under the photographs in your family's album. A picture may be worth a thousand words, but a few carefully chosen ones beneath it increase its value tremendously. Cross out the messages on greeting cards and write your own. It's your mother's birthday, your father's Father's Day, your big sister's graduation; don't let someone else tell them how you feel. Write notes to your friends and pass them in class (but don't get caught). I once fell in love with a girl in driver's education. We had a clandestine correspondence on the wrappers of Hershey bars. Our romance was conducted in writing, and our kisses tasted like chocolate.

You don't need a laptop or an iMac to write. As my Auntie Hankie says, "Charles Dickens did just fine with a quill pen."

I began this chapter by saying that writing is fun. I never said it was easy. It takes courage and confidence, both of which sometimes fail us. Ideas don't always come, but distractions do. The first sentence can be as frightening as a first kiss, and we're often stumped by where the comma goes or how to form the plural of *piano*. But these are obstacles that someone else (or the English language itself) put in your way, not you. Maybe you had a teacher who wasn't paying enough attention when you took a chance and read her your story. Maybe your older brother wasn't thinking when he sneered at your poem. Maybe you have parents or other relatives who are writers, and you're so intimidated by how well they do it, you're afraid to try. Or maybe you have a mild case of dyslexia and got so many D's and F's on spelling tests, you've been conditioned to think of yourself as bad at English.

It's time to get reconditioned. The most important step in honoring thy reader is honoring thyself. Silence those voices that tell you you can't write. Set aside a quiet, uncluttered space and a calm, uninterrupted span of time. Don't be intimidated by other writers; be inspired by them. Ignore anyone who snickers at your work, but if a reader takes the time to offer helpful criticism, listen to it; learn from it. And if you do have mild dyslexia or some other neurological reason for failing your spelling tests, get help, but don't let it get in the way.

Writing is a challenge, not a chore. Just as it's a challenge to ski a black diamond trail for the first time, it's hard to get that first sentence down on paper. But when you look up the steep slope you've just conquered, don't you want to ski it again? Sure you'll fall, you'll get snow in places you *thought* were well covered. But if you pick yourself up, dust yourself off, and get back on the trail, you'll find that the process is actually part of the fun. So don't be afraid of that empty white page: it's just a mountain of fresh snow waiting to be skied.

Two

Thou Shalt Not Waste Words

ONE OF THE HEROES OF MY CHILDHOOD was Gilligan, the first mate of the S.S. *Minnow*. He was a buffoon, a klutz, and a scapegoat. But he was also a gifted translator of convoluted English into clear words.

> PROFESSOR: I believe the lagoon is rife with savory
> crustaceans.
> GILLIGAN: Yeah, and it has a lot of good shellfish too.
> PROFESSOR: Perhaps we should employ our seafood
> procurement apparatus to obtain the
> basis for our evening repast.
> GILLIGAN: Yeah, and maybe we should go fishing
> for dinner.

These apparently dim-witted restatements of the obvious would usually provoke a smack on the head from the Skipper's cap, along with the sarcastic "Thanks a lot, Gilligan." But although he was the frequent brunt of island humor, Gilligan deserves our praise for keeping things simple.

If I could authorize my students to arrest word wasters, our jails would be overflowing with politicians. Have you ever heard a debate moderator tell a candidate, "You've still got thirty seconds left to answer the question"? Have you ever turned on C-SPAN and heard silence? A bill written by a congressperson can run five hundred pages long. It's a wonder that the stop signs in Washington, D.C. don't read, AT THIS TIME IT IS ADVISABLE TO REDUCE YOUR TRAVELING SPEED TO A RATE OF 0 MILES PER HOUR.

Is it necessary to write "at the present time" when a simple "now" will do? Is working "twenty-four hours a day all day long" more impressive than "working all day?" Why do people write, "The votes in favor of the amendment were not as many in number as those against it," when they could just as easily, and much more effectively, write, "The amendment didn't pass"?

We waste words for two reasons: we take them for granted, and we are surrounded by compulsive word wasters who think that they sound more important if they use more words. I'm not arguing for a dumbing down of English. Unlike the trucker who gives Tom Joad a ride in Chapter 1 of *The Grapes of Wrath,* I don't get mad when I hear "a guy use big words." I like big words. I like them in the dictionary, which makes excellent bedtime or bathroom reading; I like them in books; I even like them in my ear when used by a clear-thinking speaker. It's the unnecessary words that I mind, the ones that make a sentence feel like an overstuffed couch, easy to sit in, hard to get up from.

How can we keep our sentences firm? We can start by noticing the difference between wasteful and thrifty language:

WASTEFUL	THRIFTY
during the time that	while
all kinds of	(specify what kinds)
the writer who wrote	the writer of
it is my personal opinion that	I think/I believe
many in number	many
at this point in time	now
blue in color	blue
same exact	same
the month of March	March
consensus of opinion	consensus
in the event of an emergency	in an emergency
in this day and age	today/nowadays
come in contact with	meet
in view of the fact that/due to the fact that	because
give consideration to	consider
the issue under discussion at the present time	the present issue
was unaware of the fact that	didn't know
as to whether	whether
referred to as	called
I thought to myself	I thought
whole entire	whole OR entire (not both)

We can also be aware of who wastes words and who saves them:

WORD WASTERS	WORD SAVERS
Anyone on C-SPAN	Newspaper editorials
All presidential candidates	The DMV instruction manual
Attorneys billing by the hour	The National Weather Service daily forecast
Anyone allowed to speak at a board meeting	Proverbs and haiku poems
Up-talkers (you know who you are?)	Motorcycle cops
Instruction manuals, translated from Scandinavian languages, for assemble-it-yourself furniture	Myths and fairy tales
Street preachers of all persuasions	Comic strips
Valedictorians or other speakers at a high school graduation	Advertisements (but beware of subliminal seduction)
Distinguished lecturers, particularly those paid by the word	The headlines on National Public Radio
School principals, particularly when you've done something wrong	Politicians, but only when they've done something wrong
Students who summarize book plots by telling you the whole story	Movie summaries in *TV Guide*

I have to admit I have a weakness for weather. Maybe it's because I live in Southern California, a region stamped with sunshine three hundred days a year. If I lived in the Midwest and had to dig my tires out of the snow every time we ran out of diapers, I might curse the very elements that I crave here in L.A. But there is something about an approaching storm—maybe it's the promise of change—that sends me to the California section of the *Los Angeles Times,* where two of my passions come together: weather and words.

A potent storm system will invade Oregon and Washington today, spreading rainfall and cooler air across the western U.S. A cold front sliding into the northern Plains and the upper Midwest will trigger widespread showers from the Dakotas to the Great Lakes region. An upper-level weather disturbance will approach the central and southern Plains, setting off scattered thunderstorms in both zones. High pressure lingering off the New England coast will promote mostly sunny skies and mild conditions across the Northeast states. Partly to mostly cloudy skies, however, will cover the South.

Five swift sentences paint the weather picture for the nation. The words are carefully chosen and never repeated. Muscular verbs like *invade, trigger, promote,* and *cover* energize the forecast. A cold front is "sliding into the northern Plains"; high pressure is "lingering" off the New England coast. The language here is economical and effective, a model of fine writing that you should read every day, whether you live in predictable Southern California or tornado-prone Kansas.

Are there any good movies on TV tonight? Try reading the teaser summary of a movie before watching it. In your newspaper's TV listings, your cable guide, or *TV Guide,* you will find excellent examples of lean, efficient writing:

The Grapes of Wrath (1940). John Ford's Oscar-winning version of the Steinbeck novel about destitute Oklahoma farmers migrating West.

Poltergeist (1982). Chiller about a family whose home is invaded by supernatural forces.

Notting Hill (1999). A Hollywood screen goddess falls for an unassuming British bookstore owner while in London to promote her latest film.

You can be sure that these summaries were not crafted by politicians in their spare time.

Every ten years or so in California, we have a drought and are forced to conserve water. At first it's annoying to have to take shorter showers, use a rake instead of the hose to clear our driveways, or rely on our imaginations instead of the running faucet to help us pee. But after a while we adapt to the short supply of water; we even surprise ourselves by our clever ideas for conservation.

Wouldn't it be interesting if every ten years or so we had a word shortage too? Street preachers' mouths would miraculously run dry. Your parents would run out of words in the middle of a lecture. Your teachers would be forced to cut their lessons in half (and you'd be able to take fewer notes). Maybe the state of the union would improve if the State of the Union had to be delivered in less than an hour.

Eight Ways to Save Words

1. *Think Before You Write*

At UC Berkeley all of my professors were reasonably intelligent people. Some were even brilliant, but very few were first-rate writers. One professor I had, Martin Jay, gave a course on European intellectual history. He would stand at a lectern before a crowd of seventy-five or so students and read a handwritten lecture from a yellow legal pad. He had a strong voice, a handsome though not often seen smile, and a confidence that made us listen carefully to what he had to say. But it wasn't his voice, his smile, or his confidence that kept us spellbound for an hour and a half each Tuesday afternoon. It was his writing.

Martin Jay wasted no words. His train of thought never got derailed. He had written out his lectures in advance, not the night before, not the year before, but sometime in between. When he stepped up to the lectern, legal pad in hand, he was fully prepared, and we, his students, were fully relaxed: we knew we were in safe hands. At the end of the quarter the packed lecture hall erupted in applause, and our professor's smile finally came out.

Good clear writing comes from good clear thinking. The ink in your pen, like the blood in your veins, is a precious and vital commodity. Before you part with it, plan for it. Not only will you save words, you'll earn yourself a roar of applause.

2. *Use the Active Voice*

Once a month I receive the *Berkeley Wellness Letter,* a newsletter promoting good health. I've yet to read an issue that doesn't urge us to lead active lives. Active people, the researchers tell us, accomplish more and live longer than passive people.

The same is true of an active sentence. An active sentence lives longer and accomplishes more in the reader's mind. Active sentences emphasize the verb. In passive sentences the verb is deemphasized. Read the following examples and decide which you prefer:

PASSIVE	ACTIVE
A bake sale was organized by the students.	The students organized a bake sale.
The game was won by the underdogs.	The underdogs won the game.
The baton was twirled by the cheerleader.	The cheerleader twirled the baton.

What matters more, the bake sale or the fact that the students organized it? *Was organized by* slouches its way through the sentence and wastes two extra words (*was* and *by*). *Organized* zips through. Similarly, if the underdogs won the game, we should make them the stars of the sentence, just as we should marvel at the cheerleader, not her baton.

Sometimes you have to use the passive voice. *The earthquake destroyed my house* is an active sentence, but it emphasizes the earthquake at the expense of the house. *My house was destroyed by the earthquake* places your house—or what's left of it—at center stage where it belongs. Likewise, if you are filling out a police report because your car disappeared, it is better to write *My car was stolen* than *Someone stole my car.*

3. *Choose Vigorous Verbs*

Vigorous verbs carry a sentence alone; lazy ones need adverbs to get the job done. The following chart displays lazy verbs and their more muscular alternatives:

LAZY	MUSCULAR
speak softly	whisper/mutter/mumble
speak loudly	yell/trumpet/bellow/thunder
hold tightly	clench/clasp/cling
eat quickly	scarf/gobble/devour/inhale
drive rapidly	speed/careen/zoom
go slowly	meander/crawl/inch
go into	enter/brave/plunge into
start up	launch/begin/commence
sing poorly	croak/wail/screech
look at	examine/regard/observe/ study
give up	surrender/yield/forfeit

Beginning writers tend to use beginning verbs. It isn't your fault; you simply haven't been listening or reading long enough to meet the more sophisticated or elaborate verbs of the world. If you want to expand your arsenal of verbs—and all other words—become a word hunter. Add new words to your Vocabulary Friends Phone Book; get intimate with them; use them in a sentence; write them on index cards and flash them at yourself several times a day. And remember, don't be shy when wooing new words: they'll never turn you down when you ask for a date, and they'll never get jealous if you go out with other words.

4. *Lose Pretty Adjectives and "Duh" Adverbs*

Make friends with adjectives, but don't spent too much time with them: they can be a bad influence. A few well-placed adjectives can spice up a drab sentence, but too many will nauseate your reader. If the forest is green, why gunk it up with more green by writing, *The verdant emerald forest enveloped us in a cloak of green*? An egg is already oval, and oval is already a shape, so don't write, *She had an oval-shaped head like an egg*. If someone's hair *cascades* down her back, it doesn't have to be *flowing hair that cascades down her back*; the word *cascade* already flows; add *flowing,* and the meaning gets washed away.

"Duh" adverbs are adverbs whose meaning is already clear from the verb they modify. It isn't necessary to speed swiftly across the road; have you ever seen anyone speed slowly? If the rain is pelting the sidewalk, it needn't pelt it violently; *pelt* is already a violent word.

Consider the following sentences and their improvements. You can apply the same editing technique to your own writing.

SENTENCE WITH "DUH" ADVERBS OR PRETTY ADJECTIVES	REVISED SENTENCE WITHOUT
Jane asked politely, "May I please go to the bathroom?"	"May I please go to the bathroom?" Jane asked. (*May* and *please* are polite enough.)
The angry driver blared his horn loudly.	The angry driver blared his horn. (*Blare* already suggests *loud*.)
We searched frantically and nervously for our lost puppy that we couldn't find.	We searched frantically for our lost puppy. (*Lost* means *couldn't be found*; *frantically* and *nervously* carry the same idea. Both can be cut.)
We were totally delighted by your absolutely hilarious story that you wrote.	We were delighted by your funny story. (There's no such thing as *partially delighted*; you are either delighted or not. *Your* story means that *you wrote* it. And *hilarious* is too strong an adjective next to *delighted*.)
The boy rode his bicycle perilously close to the precipitous cliff.	The boy rode his bicycle perilously close to the cliff. (All *cliffs* are *precipitous*.)

5. *Weed Out Timid Words*

Timid words are a waste of mind. If you are smart enough to have an opinion, observant enough to write a description, or angry enough to voice a complaint, then remove the mufflers from your writing. Adverbs like *somewhat, slightly, a bit, quite, a little, kind of, rather,* and *very* do nothing but limit the confidence of a writer and the impact of his words.

TIMID (AND WORDY)	CONFIDENT (AND LEAN)
This woman has kind of dark hair that is somewhat wavy. Her eyes remind me a little bit of blueberries that seem to be floating in quite small pools of milk.	This woman has dark and wavy hair. Her eyes look like blueberries floating in pools of milk.
Mary's face is sort of curved and kind of squat like a pumpkin.	Mary's face is curved and squat like a pumpkin.
The rule against makeup seems very unfair. It places rather harsh limitations on our freedom of expression and for apparently no good reason. We feel quite certain that our parents will support our protest of this new policy.	The rule against makeup unjustly limits our freedom of expression. We are certain our parents will join our protest of this harsh new policy.

6. *Eliminate Excessive* Is*'s (and all other forms of the verb* to be*)*

Is *is* a verb? Yes, it is. But is *is* a strong verb or a weak verb? *Is* is a weak verb. *Is* is usually in the way of good writing. Is there a solution to the *is* problem? Indeed there is. The solution is to get rid of *is* whenever *is* is inessential.

EXCESSIVE *IS*'S	ESSENTIAL *IS*'S
Floyd Fishbone is the nation's leading expert on fly-fishing. Floyd is ninety years old.	Floyd Fishbone, the nation's leading expert on fly-fishing, is ninety.
	(We combined the sentences and lost one *is*.)
Her hair is like a rainbow. Her nose is like a button on a winter coat. Her lips are like pink pillows on a freshly made bed.	Her hair resembles a rainbow, her nose a button on a winter coat. Her lips puff out like pink pillows on a freshly made bed.
	(We replaced *is* with *resembles,* a verb strong enough to handle the first two sentences at once. Then we chose *puff out,* a more vivid verb than *are like,* to sharpen the description of her lips.)

EXCESSIVE *IS*'S	ESSENTIAL *IS*'S
I love my dog. She is mischievous. She is a terrier. She is also very cute.	I love my mischievous terrier. She is very cute. (We eliminated two *is*'s and the word *dog*. A terrier is a dog, and the second two sentences belong as one.)

7. *Make Friends with Phrases*

At some point your English teacher probably mentioned the word *phrase*. He wasn't trying to scare you; he was giving you a technique to energize your writing. A phrase is a group of words without a subject-verb combination. One type of phrase that can help you save words is a participial phrase, which begins with the present or past participle of a verb. The present participle is the *ing* form and can be used to suggest action: *Opening the closet door, I had the eerie sensation that I was not alone.* Similarly, the past participle (the form that follows *has/have/had,* as in *had eaten*) can launch a good descriptive phrase: *Eaten twice a day, seaweed can help you swim faster.*

Both these sentences express an idea that could have been stated in more words: *While I was opening the closet door, I had the eerie sensation that I was not alone* and *When you eat it twice a day, seaweed can help you swim faster.* Using participial phrases, we were able to save a total of six words.

We can also use participial phrases to combine two sentences: *The Constitution of the United States was written in 1787. It continues to be a successful blueprint for our government.* If we start with

Written in 1787 (a past participial phrase), we can join the two sentences as follows: *Written in 1787, the Constitution of the United States continues to be a successful blueprint for our government.*

Another type of phrase you may find useful is the absolute phrase. An absolute phrase modifies a whole sentence: *The storm having slackened, we were able to dig our car out of the snow.* The absolute phrase *The storm having slackened* gets the sentence off to a rolling start and saves the word *since*, as in *Since the storm had slackened, we were able to dig our car out of the snow.* My high school English teacher, George Schoenman, loved absolute phrases and would give us bonus points whenever we used one in a sentence, his reward a powerful incentive for us all. In the sentence you just read, the absolute phrase comes at the end, after the comma: *his reward a powerful incentive for us all.* I could have changed the comma to a period and written a second sentence: *His reward was a powerful incentive to us all,* but the absolute phrase makes a crisp ending to a single sentence, and I'm still trying to get bonus points from George.

Here is a chart to show how phrases can help you save words:

WASTEFUL (WITHOUT PHRASES)	FRUGAL (WITH PHRASES)
While he was racing after the bus, Johnny slipped on a patch of ice and slid so fast that he got a speeding ticket.	Racing after the bus, Johnny slipped on a patch of ice and slid so fast that he got a speeding ticket.

WASTEFUL (WITHOUT PHRASES)	FRUGAL (WITH PHRASES)
	(The participial phrase *racing after the bus* lets us eliminate the clunky *While he was.*)
J. D. Salinger has seldom been seen since the 1963 publication of *The Catcher in the Rye*. Salinger remains a mysterious figure.	Seldom seen since the 1963 publication of *The Catcher in the Rye*, J. D. Salinger remains a mysterious figure. (Using a past participial phrase, we combined the two sentences.)
In 1941 President FDR delivered his Four Freedoms speech. Its theme remains an enduring beacon of hope for us all.	In 1941 President FDR delivered his Four Freedoms speech, its theme an enduring beacon of hope for us all. (The absolute phrase lets us combine the two sentences and eliminate the verb *remains.*)

8. *Rewrite—Rewrite—Rewrite*

"The only thing worse than writing a composition is rewriting it," a student once remarked. I like this quote because it carries an often-glossed-over truth about writing: it's hard work. It isn't just creativity blasted all over a piece of paper and then handed in. It's a series of steps that begins with careful planning of what you want to express and ends only when you've expressed it in the most effective way possible. All writers, from bathroom-stall poets to professionals, can benefit from a second, third, and fourth draft. (I'm on my fifth.)

In ninth grade I had to write an analysis of *Jane Eyre*. My Auntie Hankie, a professional writer, offered to sit down with me and do a blue pencil draft of the paper.

> Brontë reveals ~~a considerable part~~ much of Mr. Rochester's character through his dialogue. ~~From~~ Rochester's words, ~~one becomes familiar with~~ convey his personality, his views on life, and his feelings for other people.
>
> When Rochester is ~~first~~ introduced ~~in the story~~, he has just ~~taken~~ a fallen off ~~of~~ his horse and ~~Jane Eyre~~ is trying to help him. He does not want ~~Jane~~ her to know he is her employer. Since they haven't met, ~~Jane has not yet been acquainted with Mr. Rochester and~~ Jane assumes that she is helping a total stranger. She inquires of the ailing man if he ~~is acquainted with~~ knows a Mr. Rochester to which he replies, " 'No, I have never seen him.' "
>
> Mr. Rochester ~~has an~~ 's object ~~in mind. He wishes~~ is to put off his meeting with Jane ~~to a later date~~ so that they can be introduced formally. ~~One sees that~~ His evasiveness suggests that Mr. Rochester is capable of being somewhat mysterious ~~and secretive~~.

"What's a blue pencil draft?" I asked her.

"It's what an editor does to a manuscript."

"Is it legal?"

She laughed. "Of course it's legal. Come on, I'll show you."

I brought her my analysis—all forty-three pages of it. We sat at her dining room table, my aunt with her pencil and I with a growing dread of what she would do with it. I watched in awe as she cut a clear blue path through my tangled sentences, leaving in the essential words and lining out the waste. Soon I realized that she wasn't butchering what I wrote; she was liberating it. And though I didn't know it at the time, she was giving me my first lesson in how to write:

When you do a second draft to kick out the clutter, keep in mind that you aren't just rewriting yourself; you are rewriting all the word wasters who came before you. Your step back is actually a step forward in the evolution of humankind. You are helping to break a cycle of unclear thinking and overweight phrasing that began with the first long-winded senator in ancient Rome and hasn't ended yet. If you stop wasting words, your little brothers and sisters will stop wasting them too. Who knows? Maybe in thirty years congressional debates on C-SPAN might actually enthrall us. Graduation speakers might be paid a bonus for all the words they *don't* use. And Gilligan's inaugural address will be only twenty minutes long.

Three

Thou Shalt Not Kill Thy Sentences

HAVE YOU EVER HEARD THE EXPRESSION "Don't kill the messenger"? It comes from ancient Greece, long before e-mail, Morse code, or movable type. If you wanted to send a message to someone, you had to have it sent—and spoken—by a human being, your messenger.

Being a messenger was a risky job. If the message you were told to deliver happened to be a good one—say, your Athenian general had just throttled the Spartans—you would be rewarded with a lavish feast, some nuggets of gold, and an instant promotion. If, on the other hand, your Athenian general had just surrendered, you would be killed on the spot.

You might think that over time a kinder, gentler system for delivering messages would have evolved, but it hasn't. True, we no longer use human beings to "run and tell so-and-so such-and-such"; now we send our messages over the Internet, through the postal service, or via pagers and cell phones. Yet we're still killing our messengers every day, because every sentence we write is a messenger for our thoughts. And if that messenger is unclear, undisciplined, or incomplete, it will be DOA—dead on arrival. So in order to stop killing our messengers, we're going to spend a chapter on promoting and maintaining the health of our sentences. We'll start by cutting them open to see what's inside.

Anatomy of a Sentence

After *How long does it have to be?*, *Can I go to the bathroom?*, and *Do we have to write that down?*, the fourth most frequently asked question in a classroom is *Are we ever going to use this stuff?* If I had to choose which of these questions is the most valid, the last would easily win. Learning by rote—that is, memorizing information without understanding why—can be beneficial when you are in kindergarten through fifth grade. But by sixth or seventh grade and for the rest of your life, you are sophisticated enough to demand an explanation for everything you learn. Some teachers find it tedious to teach the Pythagorean theorem, let alone explain its relevance to the "real world," but I've found that by explaining the relevance of something, you give someone a reason to learn it.

Why bother learning what a simple, compound, complex, or compound-complex sentence is? By learning the different types of sentences, you will be able to see patterns in your own writing and ways to improve it. A lesson on how to distinguish between an independent clause and a dependent one sounds like a form of torture, but it is really a form of training. Independent clauses have one kind of rhythm, dependent clauses another; by learning to alternate between the two, you can conduct your sentences like musical instruments and give pleasure to the reader's ear. You shouldn't learn what a dangling modifier or a split infinitive is just for the sake of doing grammar exercises; you should learn to identify these insidious sentence-killers so that you can remove them from your writing just as you would remove a tic from your arm. Stopping run-ons and fixing fragments might not seem like the straightest path to a steady job, but your writing suffer from both of these ailments, and the sooner we cure them, the better your chances are of landing not just any job but one with health insurance.

Even if, the moment you graduate from high school, you're planning to run as fast and as far as you can from an English class, you'll never outrun the need to write. Scientists write papers explaining the results of their experiments. Mathematicians write treatises on word problems. Artists write letters to foundations for grant money. Actors hope to write their memoirs someday. And in the Age of the Internet, everybody writes e-mails, instant messages, and chatroom repartee. In fact, nowadays the first impression you make may be not with a smile but with a sentence.

Subjects and Predicates

Babies eat dead bugs for dinner.
Spiders wear large red hats.
Firefighters sleep in cribs.

A sentence can be divided into two basic parts: subject and predicate. The subject tells whom or what the sentence is about. In the first sentence, the subject is *babies*; in the second it's *spiders*; and in the third it's *firefighters*. The predicate tells what the subject does, is, or is like. *Eat dead bugs for dinner, wear large red hats,* and *sleep in cribs* are the predicates of sentences 1, 2, and 3, respectively. Now, why do you have to know what a subject or a predicate is? The answer is that if you don't have one of each, you don't have a sentence, which means one more dead messenger.

You may have noticed that in the three sentences above, the subjects and predicates seem to have gotten jumbled. But it all depends on your point of view. A baby who encounters a dead insect during his trans–living room crawl might, if he's hungry enough, stop and swallow. A spider trapped by a red paper cup might be described as wearing a large red hat. And a firefighter, after battling flames in someone's home, might be so exhausted that he decides to curl up in the most convenient bed possible— the crib from which he's just rescued a sleeping infant.

If my logic sounds outlandish, feel free to rearrange the subjects and predicates as follows:

> *Spiders eat dead bugs for dinner.*
> *Firefighters wear large red hats.*
> *Babies sleep in cribs.*

All the sentences above have one-word subjects, which makes them easy to spot. Can you find the subject of the following sentence:

Last night a three-headed horse with half a tail woke me with his loud whinny.

Since subjects and predicates are forced to live together in the same sentence, sometimes they need a little privacy. We can do them a favor by dropping a privacy curtain between the two. The place to drop this privacy curtain is just to the left of the verb:

Last night a three-headed horse with half a tail | woke me with his loud whinny.

Everything to the left of the privacy curtain is the subject; everything to its right is the predicate. Now the subjects and predicates can take off all their clothes and stand, like Adam and Eve, in all their simplicity. What woke me with his loud whinny? *A three-headed horse.* Can we undress that subject even more? Sure, we can. The naked subject is *horse.*

You can undress the predicate too. *Woke me with his loud whinny* is the complete predicate. By stripping it of all the inessential words, we reduce it to the simple predicate *woke.* The basic subject-verb combination, then, is *horse-woke.*

Try undressing this one:

The melodious sound of a whippoorwill surprised and delighted the children.

The privacy curtain should be dropped to the left of the first verb:

The melodious sound of a whippoorwill | surprised and delighted the children.

What surprised and delighted the children? Sound. *Sound* is the basic subject. What did it do? *Surprised and delighted* is the basic predicate.

Being able to recognize subjects and predicates is the first step to recognizing the pattern of an English sentence. Once you see the pattern in your own sentences, you'll know when it's time to break it, to mix things up for the sake of keeping your sentences lively—and alive.

Sally Marks, a daredevil in my sister's class, rode her scooter to the zoo. Jimmy Lemmo, the heartthrob of the school, rode his too.

Here we have two sentences that repeat the same predicate. We can liven things up by letting Sally and Jimmy share the predicate of a new sentence:

Sally Marks, a daredevil in my sister's class, and Jimmy Lemmo, the heartthrob of the school, rode their scooters to the zoo.

Just for fun, let's drop a privacy curtain between the subject and predicate:

Sally Marks, a daredevil in my sister's class, and Jimmy Lemmo, the heartthrob of the school, | rode their scooters to the zoo.

Now if Sally and Jimmy want to get better acquainted, no one will bother them.

What's a Clause, Anyway?

Ask a group of children what a clause is, and they'll tell you it's a fat guy who gets stuck in the chimney on Christmas Eve. And that's a fairly accurate definition of a *Claus*. But a *clause* (small *c*, *e* at the end) is a group of words that includes a conjugated verb (that is, a verb paired up with a subject). Some clauses can stand alone and make sense: these are called independent clauses. In the sentence *The boy left home because he couldn't stand the cooking, The boy left home* is the independent clause (it stands on its own). *Because he couldn't stand the cooking,* however, doesn't make sense on its own. It depends on the first half of the sentence to make it clear, so we call it a dependent clause.

Read the following sentence and see if you can pick out the independent and dependent clauses.

Whenever it rains, my aunt forgets her umbrella.

To test a clause for its dependence or independence, pull it out of the sentence and slap a period on it. Does it make sense on its own? If so, it's an independent clause; if not, it's a dependent one. *Whenever it rains.* That's a tease: it leaves the reader waiting for more information. It's an incomplete thought and begins with the subordinating word *whenever.* It must be a dependent clause. *My aunt forgets her umbrella.* That's an independent clause: it makes sense by itself.

Simple, Compound, and Complex Sentences

One hallmark of good writing is variety. Very young children aren't interested in variety. They like the same foods (pasta and Cheerios), the same clothes ("No, Daddy, I want to wear my blue shirt again"), and the same bedtime routine (brush teeth, read books, bed). But somewhere around the age of five or six, a child's curiosity awakens, and a piece of salmon actually gets eaten. This milestone marks the dawn of a new developmental era, as the child is no longer satisfied with the familiar but craves the exotic—in stories, clothing, friends, and food.

Readers crave variety too. If all your sentences are alike, they may appeal to your very young siblings, but your audience most likely consists of an older, more demanding crowd. By knowing what simple, compound, and complex sentences are, you can make sure that you have a good mix of all three in your paragraphs and thereby keep your readers awake.

A simple sentence has one subject and one predicate. Even if the subject has two nouns to it, the sentence is still simple.

> *George and Martha were lying on the floor in a puddle of water, dead.*

The subject is *George and Martha*; the predicate is *were lying on the floor in a puddle of water, dead*. Likewise, the predicate can have two verbs, but the sentence is still simple: *Their fishbowl had fallen to the floor and shattered. Had fallen* and *shattered* are the two verbs that make up the predicate. An easy way to spot a simple sentence is to count the number of privacy curtains it has. A sentence with only one privacy curtain is a simple sentence.

A compound sentence is made of two or more simple sentences joined by commas and conjunctions or semicolons. In a compound sentence you will always find at least two privacy curtains—that is, two *separate* subject-verb combinations.

> *George and Martha | could swim, but the puddle of water | was too shallow.*

George and Martha could swim is the first independent clause; *the puddle of water was too shallow* is the second. They are joined by a comma and *but*.

When you combine an independent clause and a dependent clause, you get a complex sentence.

> *George and Martha couldn't walk away because they are fish.*

The independent clause is *George and Martha couldn't walk away*; the dependent clause is *because they are fish*.

Some sentences really strut their stuff by joining a compound sentence with a complex one. We call these compound-complex sentences, but although they have a fancy name, they're really quite simple. (You just read one. The comma *but* makes the sentence compound; the dependent clause *although they have a fancy name* makes it complex; put them together, and you have a compound-complex sentence.)

How We *Are* Going to Use This Stuff

Let's read a few passages from a famous book to see how the author varies his simple, compound, complex, and compound-complex sentences:

When writing about oneself, one must strive to be truthful. [simple] Truth is more important than modesty. [simple] I must tell you, therefore, that it was I and I alone who had the idea for the great and daring Mouse Plot. [compound-complex] We all have our moments of brilliance and glory, and this was mine. [compound]

This is an excerpt from *Boy: Tales of Childhood* by Roald Dahl. In setting up his story about how he and four friends used a dead mouse to avenge the villainous candyseller, Mrs. Pratchett, Dahl includes a variety of sentence structures to create a leisurely beginning. But notice how he adds a little speed:

Thwaites handed me the mouse. [simple] I put it into my trouser pocket. [simple] Then the five of us left the school, crossed the village green and headed for the sweet-shop. [simple—one subject doing three verbs] We were tremendously jazzed up. [simple] We felt like a gang of desperados out to rob a train or blow up the sheriff's office. [simple]

Five simple sentences in a row: boom, boom, boom, boom, boom. A whole page of simple sentences would be tedious, but Dahl quickly shifts to dialogue, a good source of variety, then goes back to mixing things up:

I kept to the rear of the group, and when I saw Mrs. Pratchett turn her head away for a couple of seconds to fish a Sherbet Sucker out of the box, I lifted the heavy glass lid of the Gobstopper jar and dropped the mouse in. [compound-complex] Then I replaced the lid as silently as possible. [simple] My heart was thumping like mad, and my hands had gone all sweaty. [compound]

Notice that the longest sentence, the compound-complex one, is the most suspenseful. It takes time for a boy to sneak a dead mouse into a jar of candy, and Dahl uses a string of clauses and phrases to give his sentence—and the boy—enough time to do it.

The passage ends with a trio of simple sentences to suggest the triumph of the narrator: "I felt like a hero. I *was* a hero. It was marvelous to be so popular."

Why bother learning the different kinds of sentences? It's not about exams. It's not about torture. It's about excellence and how to achieve it.

Diseases and Cures

Surgery isn't for everyone. Most people would rather view the *outside* of the human body than the *inside*. But there is a kind of surgery you can learn that won't gross you out, and it will take only the rest of this chapter to get certified. We'll try not to kill anyone. We might save lives. We're certain to save words. There will be no blood in our operating room, just ink. Like heart surgeons, we'll improve circulation—the circulation of ideas. Like brain surgeons, we'll remove anything that interferes with clear thinking. And like plastic surgeons, we'll make our patients wrinkle-free. By the time you graduate, you will be fully qualified to do surgery on an ailing English sentence. But please beware that while *The Pen Commandments* can authorize you to perform such operations, you will have to purchase your own malpractice insurance. For the time being I suggest that you limit your surgery to your own words.

Misplaced, Dangling, and Indecisive Modifiers

One of the most common symptoms of a diseased English sentence is that dreadful ear-twitcher, the misplaced modifier. A modifier is a fancy word for an adjective or adverb—words that add something to other words. A modifier can be just one word (*beautiful, quickly*) or several words (*with braces, which I've never eaten*). To avoid confusion, make sure that your modifiers land in the right place.

A man climbed Mount Everest on my street.

Well, unless you live in the Himalayas, Mount Everest isn't on your street. And unless the man who climbed Everest is uncommonly strong, chances are he didn't pick up that famous peak and move it to your neighborhood. As a sentence surgeon, you could cut the modifier and stitch it closer to its target noun:

A man on my street climbed Mount Everest.

Here's another sentence with a misplaced modifier:

Eaten past the expiration date, we got sick from the sandwich.

In a logical world, we're not the ones who get eaten; the sandwich is. A little corrective surgery repairs the problem: *Eaten past the expiration date, the sandwich made us sick.* Or *We got sick from eating a sandwich past its expiration date.*

Here's another:

Chasing a ball into the street, the delivery truck almost hit the puppy.

According to the sentence, the delivery truck was chasing a ball into the street. I do know some drivers who get their road kicks by trying to mow down animals, pedestrians, and toys. But it's more likely—and more logical—that the *puppy* was chasing the ball into the street, and the truck swerved. A good sentence surgeon will do a noun transplant to make the sentence clear:

Chasing a ball into the street, Rover was nearly flattened by the delivery truck.

Like the misplaced modifier, the dangling modifier is a sign of a diseased sentence. When something dangles, it looks like it's about to fall because it has nothing secure to latch on to. In a sentence with a dangling modifier, the writer knows which word the modifier is supposed to latch on to but forgot to include that word in the sentence:

Even with years of experience, Climax is a difficult run to ski.

Who's got the experience here, Climax (the trail) or the skier who tackles it? This sentence would read better if it had a skier in it:

Climax is a difficult run even for experienced skiers.

or

Even with years of experience, a skier faces a difficult challenge on Climax.

The next awkward sentence, one of my favorites, comes from a student's paper:

Standing in my room, a naked lady suddenly walked by.

Lucky kid, right? Not exactly. The naked lady wasn't standing in his room. *He* was standing in his room and saw, from his window, a naked lady walking by. If we cut and move the modifier, we get a clearer sentence: *Standing in my room, I saw a naked lady walk by.* Or *I was standing in my room when a naked lady suddenly walked by my window.*

At some point in your practice of sentence surgery, you might encounter indecisive modifiers. These are modifiers that can't decide which part of the sentence they belong to.

Pamela was convinced on Wednesday she would win the lottery.

Was she convinced on Wednesday, or was she going to win on Wednesday?

If you see (or write) a sentence with an indecisive modifier, surgically insert the word *that* before or after the modifier, to make your meaning clear.

Pamela was convinced that she'd win the lottery on Wednesday.

Another cure for indecisive modifiers is to write around them.

How we got Lucy to stop barking completely amazes us.

Did we get Lucy to stop barking *completely* or are we *completely* amazed? *How we got Lucy to stop barking* isn't the most elegant way to start a sentence. A smoother start might be *We were completely amazed that we got Lucy to stop barking* (if you mean you were completely amazed) or *It amazed us that we got Lucy to stop barking completely* (if she no longer makes a sound).

Split Infinitivitis

An infinitive is a phrase that starts with the word *to* and is followed by the basic form of a verb. In the sentence *We have to leave for the airport,* the infinitive phrase is *to leave.* But if we add an adverb, such as *quickly,* where should it go? Grammar books tell us not to split an infinitive, so the adverb should come after *leave* or before *to. We have quickly to leave* sounds stuffy. *We have to quickly leave* makes sense but splits the infinitive. *We have to leave quickly* is the best choice. As a rule, avoid splitting your infinitives.

There is an exception: *Star Trek.* My brother Dan was addicted to the show. Every evening from six to seven, he would lie on our family room floor, his legs propped against the TV cabinet, and let his mind and soul be sucked into the set. *Star Trek* had a great opening: that rubbery sci-fi music followed by William Shatner's confident voice: *Space, the final frontier. These are the voyages of the* Starship Enterprise, *whose five-year mission—to seek out new life and new civilization . . . To boldly go where no man has gone before.*

George Schoenman taught us never to split an infinitive. But I couldn't get the *Star Trek* motto out of my head: *to boldly go where no man has gone before.* Did Captain Kirk have bad grammar? Isn't it wrong to split an infinitive?

The answer is usually it's wrong—and sometimes it's right. The catch phrase *to boldly go where no man has gone before* sounds, well, bolder than its grammatically "proper" counterpart, *to go boldly where no man has gone before.* Occasionally a split infinitive makes sense (or a more dramatic sound), but if you are going to deliberately break the infinitive rule, be sure you've mastered it first.

Parallel Structure Disorder

Here is another type of sentence that may end up in your operating room:

> *My sister is a ballerina, a poet, and she plays the violin.*

The human mind likes a clean pattern, not a broken one. Here the pattern is noun (ballerina), noun (poet), and verb (plays the violin). The sentence misfires when you hit the verb because your ear was anticipating a third noun. Corrected, it should read:

> *My sister is a ballerina, a poet, and a violinist.*

or

My sister does ballet, writes poetry, and plays the violin.

Either approach—noun, noun, noun or verb, verb, verb—pays homage to your sister's many talents, while at the same time displaying one of *yours*: writing a sentence with parallel structure.

Pacemaker Syndrome

One night while I was in high school, I returned home from a date around midnight and was greeted by a sign on our front door:

WE'VE TAKEN DAD TO THE E.R.

MEET US THERE.

Fifteen minutes later I was watching my father's heartbeat on a monitor. An EKG (electrocardiogram) of a healthy heart looks like a series of evenly spaced *V*'s that dip below the surface of a straight line. My father's EKG had irregular spikes thrown in, and the *V*'s came sometimes too close together and sometimes too far apart. He was suffering from arrhythmia, a misfiring heart. His doctors were going to give him a mild electrical shock to get it back to normal, and a pacemaker to keep it there. It is now twenty years later, and my father's heart is beating like a metronome.

The trouble is, so are some of the sentences I read. An EKG of your writing should look completely different from one of your heart.

My brother Michael is a writer. He writes short stories. Last sum-mer he lived in Rome.

The three sentences have a kind of robotic rhythm. Read them again in a robot voice, and you'll see what I mean.

One technique we can use to enliven this rhythm is to com-bine all three sentences using an appositive:

My brother Michael, a writer of short stories, lived in Rome last summer.

The appositive *a writer of short stories* acts like a name tag for a noun, in this case the proper noun *Michael.* By pinning it on *Michael,* we turned three halting sentences into one fluid one.

Pablo Picasso was a Spanish painter. He painted Guernica. He died in 1978.

Here again, the three metronomic sentences can be combined:

Pablo Picasso, the Spanish painter of Guernica, died in 1978.

You don't have to place an appositive in the middle of a sen-tence; sometimes it belongs at the end:

My father-in-law was awarded the Croix de Guerre during World War II. The Croix de Guerre is one of France's highest military honors.

The two sentences combined read:

> *During World War II my father-in-law was awarded the Croix de Guerre, one of France's highest military honors.*

If your sentences suffer from a boring rhythm, pump them up with an appositive, a name tag for a noun.

Conjunctionitis

The opposite of a choppy sentence is a loopy one. You can hear loopy sentences tumbling out of a toddler's mouth:

> *We went to the park, and we played on the swings, and we went on the slide, and we made sand castles, and we rode the merry-go-ground, but the ice cream truck caught on fire, and we didn't have ice cream.*

An adult's response to this loopy account of a day at the park is to nod. A reader's response would be to nod off. The rhythm is so exact, so predictable, that the sentence becomes hypnotic. It also fails to highlight the highlight of the day: the ice cream truck caught on fire. This, the most dramatic and surprising detail, gets lost in the slow shuffle of *subject-verb-and, subject-verb-and, subject-verb-but, subject-verb-and.* The solution is to draw your scalpel, cut out the conjunctions, and mix things up:

> *We went to the park and played on the swings, the slide, and the merry-go-round. We didn't have any ice cream, though. While building sand castles, we noticed a cloud of black smoke on the*

other side of the park fence. Bright orange flames clawed at the sky as frantic children scattered from the ice cream truck, which had caught on fire.

Longer? Yes. Loopier? No. Livelier? You bet.

Case Studies

Run-on Randy

In my ten years of teaching, I've had all kinds of students. I've taught the giddy, the depressed, the energetic, and the sleepy. I've taught the healthy and the sick, the wealthy and the poor, the clever and the confused. I've had the sons of ambassadors, the daughters of politicians, and the grandson of Judy Garland. I've even taught a kid who had gone to the same elementary school *I* went to, where he had had *my* third-grade teacher, Mrs. Vallens.

One year a student popped up in one of my classes the likes of whom I had never seen before. His name was Randy, and the only way to describe him is to say that he entered my room right out of a cartoon. He had a high-pitched, pebbly voice that sounded like Bugs Bunny, only he was smarter if you could catch the words exploding from his mouth. On a hot afternoon, while the rest of his classmates would be drained from the previous five hours of work and forty-five minutes of lunchtime chatter, Randy would be all wound up and ready to learn. His entrances and exits left skid marks, and he charmed me like my favorite animated dog, Scooby-Doo.

Of course, now and then I had to discipline Randy. His name often appeared on the board in the penalty box or in the special class ledger reserved for the incorrigible. Once I even had to tie his legs together to keep them from starting an earthquake as he tapped his toes. But the truth is, it was a joy to have this cartoon kid in my class. On days Randy was absent, the normally brisk afternoons seemed to crawl by.

Anyone who knew Randy then knew that he talked faster than an auctioneer. Anyone who'd ever been his English teacher knew that he wrote just as fast, blazing through sentences without paying much attention to where they should pause or, more important, stop. This unrestrained enthusiasm earned Randy the nickname the *Run-on Kid*.

Here is an excerpt from his report on knights:

A kid who wanted to become a knight had to accomplish many hard tasks he had to carry his master's armor he had to stand outside all night in the cold rain, he even had to learn good table manners from the ladies of the castle.

Randy loved knights. He loved anything to do with adventure, fantasy, and heroism. When he presented the oral portion of his knights report, he brought in a slide projector and a carousel of images that he spun like a roulette wheel. When I took away the control button for the slide projector and gave it to a more leisurely student, the class was able to follow his report and voted it one of the best of the year. If there were a similar remote control that could be used to slow down Randy's arm as he wrote, I might have been able to understand his written presentation. But the only way I could rein in his run-ons was to order Randy to attend tutoring sessions after school.

"Randy," I began, "do you know what a sentence is?"

"Yeah, a sentence is a subject and a predicate."

"Good."

"Can I go?"

"Not yet, Randy. How do you know when a new sentence begins?"

"It starts with a capital letter."

"That's right—"

"Now can I go?"

"After we clear up a few things. Do you know what a run-on is?"

"A really long sentence."

"A sentence can be long without being a run-on. William Faulkner wrote sentences that lasted a whole page."

"Do I have to read his books?"

"Not now. But someday you might want to."

"Okay. Can I go?"

"Soon, Randy. I just have a few more questions for you. What's a period?"

"A dot. Like in dot-com."

"And where does a period go when you're writing a sentence?"

"At the end."

"And what happens if you forget the period at the end of a sentence?"

"It keeps going."

"Right. And what do you call that long string of words with no periods to stop it that just keeps on going and going and going?"

"The Energizer sentence."

"What do *I* call it?"

"A run-on?"

"A run-on. Good."

"Now can I go?"

"Yes, that's all for today, Randy. You may go. But go slowly."

He nodded, took a couple of deliberate steps, and then raced out the door.

Randy's next composition had one sentence and twenty-three run-ons. I ordered him back to after-school tutoring.

"Randy, do you remember our conversation about run-ons?"

"Kind of."

"Did you forget about it while writing this last composition?"

"Kind of."

I realized that Randy was an eccentric kid who would learn best from an eccentric example. So I grabbed a piece of chalk and wrote the following gibberish sentence on the board:

Spoogly naddited his glob Pixelly krumched it.

Randy read the sentence aloud and laughed. "That's funny," he said.

"Know what else it is?"

"A run-on?"

"Know why?"

Randy shook his head back and forth fast, like a dog after a bath.

"Can you draw a privacy curtain between each subject and its predicate?"

He nodded his head just as fast, then proceeded to draw two vertical lines.

The board looked like this:

Spoogly | *naddited his glob Pixelly* | *krumched it.*

"Good. *Spoogly naddited his glob.* That's one sentence. *Pixelly krumched it.* That's another."

"But there's nothing in between."

"Exactly! It's a run-on."

"How do you stop it?" he asked.

I made a drawing on the board that looked something like this:

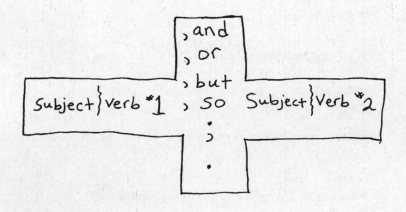

"If you have one subject-verb combination followed by another subject-verb combination, you have to slow things down by putting something in between. That something can be a *comma-and, comma-or, comma-but, comma-so, semicolon,* or *period.*"

Randy looked up at the sentence on the board. Then he rewrote it in a storm of chalk:

Spoogly naddited his glob. Pixelly krumched it.

"Is that a run-on?" he asked.

"Nope."

"Can we try another?" he asked.

I wrote a new sentence on the board:

Spoogly blagged and gippeled his blook.

Randy stared at it for a moment and then remarked, "That's not a run-on."

"Why not?"

"It's got one subject and two verbs. That's just a sentence."

"Good. Now try this:"

Pixelly tropped Spoogly's kram but Spoogly nidn't frone.

"That one's a run-on."

"Can you stop it?"

He took the chalk from my hand and added a comma before the *but.*

Pixelly tropped Spoogly's kram, but Spoogly nidn't frone.

"Looks good to me."

"So all I have to do is go through my composition and stick in commas and conjunctions, semicolons, or periods, and I'll stop my run-ons?"

"All twenty-three of them."

Randy whipped out a pen and wrote something on his arm. When he'd finished, he held up a tattoo of the diagram I'd done on the board.

"Can I go now?" he asked.

"Yes, Randy. You can go." And he screeched out of the room.

Randy still writes run-ons, but instead of twenty-three per composition, he commits a mere handful. He still talks like you're an answering machine that can take only a fifteen-second message, but when his classmates and teachers beg him to slow down, he does—for a few breaths. He is still a clever and charming kid, but now we get to enjoy his wit and charm on the page, because his sentences, like the thoughts they carry, linger long enough to be understood.

The Tallest Student I Ever Taught

Fragments were never a problem for Randy. But they were for Mindy, another of my former students. English wasn't Mindy's favorite subject. Her handwriting was small, shy almost, and seldom filled more than half a page. If you had to give it a name, the way we name fonts, it would be *hesitant, 10-point, extra light*. If you met her in person, you would marvel at the contrast between her handwriting and her height—in sixth grade, at just eleven years old, Mindy towered over the rest of us at six feet two inches tall. For Halloween she came as Marie Antoinette, in a skirt as wide as it was long.

Why were her sentences so short, then? The mere mention of a composition intimidates some students. At the sight of an empty page, their minds clam up, their eyes glaze over, and they panic. They can sit for hours and produce just a few fragmentary thoughts. In sports this phenomenon is known as "choking," and the thing they choke on is fear.

In my class students often read their work aloud. Afraid that her ideas weren't good enough, Mindy dreaded being called up. "Everyone else is such a good writer," she once said. "They'll laugh at me."

The hesitation in her writing clipped her sentences. She would begin a thought but not finish it. Subjects would appear without predicates and predicates without subjects. In a description of a fellow classmate, Mindy wrote, "Her hair is like a coconut tree. On a windy day. Brown eyes. Lots of tiny freckles. Reminds me of the dots in a dot-to-dot coloring book. Funny smile. Digs little holes in her cheeks. She is nice to look at. Nice to be friends with."

Mindy is actually a very good writer. She uses similes (she compares hair to a coconut tree, freckles to dots in a coloring book). She uses personification (the smile digs dimples in her cheeks). She also humanizes the description, makes it more emotional, by writing that her subject is pleasing to look at—and to be friends with. But her writing isn't smooth; it has the rhythm of shorthand: it sputters and stalls.

When I went over Mindy's description with her, I asked her how much time she'd spent on it. (The passage above is just an excerpt; she wrote about three-quarters of a page.) "About two hours," she said. "I wasn't sure if it was any good."

"It is good. It's very good."

She squinted at me, suspecting a lie.

"There's some very good writing here. It's just unfinished."

"I couldn't think of any more ideas."

"It doesn't need more ideas. It needs more room. It needs to breathe."

I wrote on the board Mindy's first sentence and the fragment that followed:

Her hair is like a coconut tree. On a windy day.

"What is it about her hair that reminds you of a coconut tree?" I asked.

"It's all spiky and messy. It looks like it would hurt if you touched it."

"That's an amazing image. But the way you've delivered it sounds like you aren't sure. Try putting *on a windy day* in the first sentence, then throw in those colorful adjectives you just mentioned."

She rewrote the sentence:

Her hair is all spiky and messy, like a coconut tree on a windy day.

She stood back and read.

"Like it?" I asked.

She shrugged.

"It sounds bolder that way, doesn't it?"

She nodded.

"It's a good sentence, Mindy."

She nodded again, this time with a smile.

Grammatically speaking, a sentence has to have a subject and a predicate; one without the other is a fragment. When you hear a fragment, you crinkle your eyebrows and say, "Ka-what?"

The broken-winged bird.

Ka-what?

My Uncle Charles, president of the Uncle Charles Fan Club.

Ka-what?

Cannot fly.

Ka-what?

Appointed himself to an unprecedented fifth term.

Ka-what?

The first two fragments are subjects in search of predicates. The next two are predicates missing their subjects. To correct them, add the missing part:

The broken-winged bird cannot fly.

My Uncle Charles, president of the Uncle Charles Fan Club, appointed himself to an unprecedented fifth term.

Fragments aren't just faults of grammar, though; they're confidence errors. The halting sensation they create in a writer's style is like the hesitation you might have felt the first time you rode a bike, dribbled a basketball, or stood on skis. With a little practice it's easy to spot the fragments you've written and go back and correct them. A nobler goal is to eliminate the fragments in the first place, to stop choking on your own insecurity and take a chance at being bold.

Each fall my students read a humorous story by Isaac Bashevis Singer called "The First Shlemiel." *Shlemiel* is a Yiddish word that translates, roughly, as an "unlucky and unskillful person." In the story Shlemiel's wife has to go out shopping but doesn't want Shlemiel to eat the holiday jam she is saving for Passover. She tells him there are three things he must be very careful not to do: don't wake the baby; don't let the chicken out of the house; and don't eat the pot of poison on the top shelf. Shlemiel ends up waking the baby and letting the chicken out of the house. Afraid that his wife will come home and berate him for his stupidity, Shlemiel decides to kill himself. But how to do it? After considering and rejecting various methods, he remembers the pot of poison in the kitchen and decides to eat it all. To find out what happens, you'll have to read the story.

As a companion lesson to "The First Shlemiel," I teach the kids a few expressions in Yiddish. One of their favorite Yiddish words is *chutzpah,* which translates, roughly, as "gall, guts, outrageous confidence." In *Oliver Twist,* when Oliver asks for more food, that's chutzpah. In *The Phantom Tollbooth,* when Milo steals a *but* from the Soundkeeper's fortress, that's chutzpah. In seventh grade I told my sewing teacher, Mrs. Jitlov, that I deserved to pass her class even though I couldn't sew a straight line. She asked me why I deserved to pass, and I explained that my failure wasn't my fault, wasn't even her fault; it was the fault of an educational system that overworked its teachers so much that they didn't have time to help individuals in need. My argument took advantage of overcrowding at our public school; it preyed on Mrs. Jitlov's sense of guilt; and it completely glossed over the real reason I couldn't sew—I had ditched most of her classes. But it was a bold and confident approach. It had chutzpah. And it worked!

In order to avoid writing fragments, all you need is a little chutzpah. With a little chutzpah, Mindy wouldn't have balked at her comparison between her classmate and a coconut tree. She would have been proud of her essay and read it to the class in **Ariel bold, 14-point**. Her writing would have stood as tall as she did.

At the end of the year, Mindy told me she would be attending a new school in the fall. Her family was moving to Palos Verdes, and the commute to our school would be too much for them. I asked her how she felt about changing schools, and she said she was looking forward to playing on the girls' basketball team.

"I didn't know you played," I said.

"I do."

Then her friend with the spiky hair said, "Mr. Frank, Mindy's amazing. The coach at her new school recruited her."

It wasn't Mindy's style to boast. But I sure was glad I'd found out about her secret talent.

"Mindy," I said, "will you do me a favor?"

"Sure, Mr. Frank."

"Will you save me a seat at the WBA finals in the year 2015?"

"Center court okay?"

"A few rows back."

She nodded, a proud, confident nod. I can picture her now from my center court seat a few rows back: she is an elegant Amazon floating to the net and slam-dunking the winning shot, a girl who's outgrown her fragments—a woman with chutzpah.

Four

Thou Shalt Not Pick on the Puncts

PUNCTUATION MARKS ARE GETTING MAD. They've been neglected, misused, and picked on for too long, and if we don't start treating them with respect, they'll go on strike.

A punctuation strike would be worse than an air traffic con trollers strike a janitors strike and a nurses strike combined imag ine if all of our sentences were unmarked and all our thoughts allowed to spill willynilly onto the page how would you know when one sentence ended and the next began how would your reader be able to find let alone board your train of thought our sentences would no longer communicate they would confuse the result a meltdown in communication a nervous breakdown among all human beings meanwhile the eleven marks of punctu ation twelve if you count the ellipsis would be calmly picketing in the margins of our newspapers books and essays puncts on strike puncts on strike what a sad day for humanity

Want to avoid this mess? Read on.

. (period)

*There's not much to be said about the period except that most
writers don't reach it soon enough.*

—WILLIAM ZINSSER

When I turned four and a half, my father slapped a pair of
wooden sticks on my feet and taught me how to ski. His first lesson wasn't how to plant my poles or make a turn or even ride the
chair lift. His first lesson was how to stop.

"When you want to stop, turn your skis to face uphill," he
advised. "Gravity will slow you down; then all you've got to do is
sit." This was good advice, except that I never wanted to stop.
I was a daredevil, a speed demon, a pint-size Phil Mahre—the
only thing that would stop me was the warming hut, which I
crashed into a few times before realizing that breaking the down-
hill record wasn't worth breaking my legs.

My father's technique worked. I'd hold a turn long enough
to point my skis uphill and then sit down, my butt making a perfectly round hole where it landed. As seen from the chair lift
above, this "sitzmark" at the end of my tracks looked like the
period at the end of a sentence. My first lesson in skiing was,
coincidentally, also my first lesson in punctuation.

A period ends a declarative sentence. Periods are powerful,
simple, and clear. They are the red lights of writing, the traffic
cop's upheld hand. When you come to a period, you stop, absorb
the thought of a sentence, and then read on. If it's a very long
sentence, you're glad to get to the period. If it's a very short one,

you might wish it wouldn't come so soon. (A note on typing: space twice after a period. Just as a car needs stopping distance when it comes to a red light, so the human mind needs stopping distance when it comes to the end of a sentence.)

This firm and noble mark of punctuation is also used in abbreviations. Here it acts like a retaining wall for the scrunched letters of a shortened word. *Mister* becomes *Mr.*; *Doctor* becomes *Dr.*; *Los Angeles* becomes *L.A.* If we forget the periods in our abbreviations, the letters will spill out and slide down the page, causing inestimable damage to the sentences below.

The period plays a similar role in Internet navigation. As the dot in *.com, .org, .gov,* and *.net,* it keeps all of our Web-surfing computers on a straight path.

Period Triplets: The Ellipsis (. . .)

Sometimes periods travel in threes. When they do, their function is the opposite of stopping ideas; it's to let them roll on. Three dots in a row make the *ellipsis* (. . .), the "yada, yada, yada" of punctuation. An ellipsis suggests that something has been left out or unfinished. It could mean *and so on and so forth* or *etc.* Often it indicates part of a quotation that has been skipped:

> *As it says in the Declaration of Independence, "When, in the course of human events, it becomes necessary for one people to dissolve the political bands which have connected them with another, and to assume . . . the separate but equal station to which the laws of nature and of nature's God entitle them . . . they should declare the causes which impel them to the separation."*

The two ellipses above indicate that some lines from the original Declaration have been left out.

You can also use the ellipsis to recreate a stutter or to suggest hesitation in dialogue:

> *"The coat was too big for me and . . . and T. J. said it made me look like . . . like a preacher . . . and he said since it fit him just right, he'd . . . he'd take it off my hands till I grow into it, then thataway all the guys would stop laughing at me and calling me preacher."*
>
> —MILDRED TAYLOR,
> *Roll of Thunder, Hear My Cry*

Have you ever had a thought too terrible to conclude? Maybe your parents left you in charge of your little brother or sister, and you discovered that your younger sibling had stamped the family's return address all over the silk-covered camel-back sofa. You might have turned to the guilty toddler and said, "Oh, boy! When Mom and Dad come home . . ." The ellipsis at the end of that statement shows the disappearing trail of a thought that, if carried through, would be too dreadful to pronounce, let alone print.

Notice how E. B. White, in *Charlotte's Web,* uses an ellipsis to show us that Wilbur's thought is heading for an unfortunate conclusion:

> *Wilbur heard several people make favorable remarks about Uncle's great size. He couldn't help overhearing these remarks,*

and he couldn't help worrying. "And now, with Charlotte not feeling well . . ." he thought. "Oh, dear!"

Most of your thoughts will, I hope, be printable. But when you must write something unspeakable, scatter the three dots of an ellipsis at the end of your sentence. Your reader will understand what you mean.

, (comma)

When do you use a comma? For some writers the answer is "Whenever I can." Their books tend to be over five hundred pages long. For others it's "Only when I have to." These are the Ernest Hemingways or Raymond Chandlers of the literary world—terse, tough, and popular among students the week before a book report is due. The lucky ones, those with an ear for commas, will say, "Whenever I feel one coming." These are writers like Charles Dickens, Jane Austen, E. B. White, and Roald Dahl—writers whose books may be thin or fat, easy or challenging, but whose commas always seem to hang in just the right place.

Beginning writers answer the comma question by saying they aren't sure when to use one. If *comma* were spelled *calm-a,* its purpose would be clear: to calm the reader, to slow things down just long enough for the reader to catch his breath, but not so long that he comes to a full stop. Treat a comma the way Californians treat a stop sign: roll leisurely through.

My Roommate Who Clicked

In the Kalahari Desert there are certain Bushmen who have a distinct advantage over us inhabitants of "developed" countries. They don't use just words to communicate; they click, too. Interspersed among the syllables they utter are soft clicking sounds like those a squirrel makes when chasing its mate. A typical Kalahari conversation might go something like this:

"Hey *click* brother, what do you *click* want for breakfast *click* today?"

"*Click* I'm hungry for a *click* Egg Mc *click* Muffin."

"Is the new Mc *click* Donald's open *click* yet?"

"Yes *click*. Let's go *click* right away *click*."

These could be affectionate clicks, thought-gathering clicks, angry clicks, or even questioning clicks. The possibilities are endless.

In the United States there is a tribe of suave recent college graduates who are just beginning to climb the corporate ladder, and they click, too. I know because I had one for a roommate. A typical late-afternoon conversation between us went like this:

"Hey *click* dude *click* how's it going?

"Just fine, Dave. Are you going out tonight?"

"Oh *click* yeah. I've got a date with a total babe *click* but I haven't decided where to take her yet."

"How many women are you dating these days?"

"Well *click* let me see if I can name them. There's Donna *click* Sue *click* Sabrina *click* Valerie *click* Olivia *click* Mary-Jane *click* and Mathilda."

One day I decided to transcribe Dave's speech to see if there was any pattern to his clicking. I discovered that Dave's clicks were the verbal equivalent of commas, and the remarkable thing about them was that they all landed in the right places. In English you are supposed to put a comma before the name or title of someone whom you are addressing directly. If Dave's clicks were transcribed as commas, they would have read:

Hey, dude, how's it going?

Commas belong after interjections like *oh, hey, gee,* and so on. Dave clicked right on cue:

Oh, yeah. I've got a date with a total babe, but I haven't decided where to take her yet.

Note the click before the word *but.* That's a perfect place for a comma—before the conjunction when joining two independent clauses.

He also clicked his way through the long list of ladies he was dating. In English this is called the serial comma, not because it's wanted by the FBI but because it respects the individuality of each member of a series:

There's Donna, Sue, Sabrina, Valerie, Olivia, Mary-Jane, and Mathilda.

Of course, Dave's clicks sometimes represented more than marks of punctuation. When I asked him if he'd be coming home that night, he turned to me and, adding a wink, replied, *"Click."*

Tips on Clicking (or When to Use a Comma)

The following is a succinct list of comma tips. The best way to learn them is to start clicking when you talk. If you are uncomfortable clicking, then try saying the word *comma* every time you see one.

Use a Comma . . .

1. Right before people's names or titles when addressing them directly:

   Good afternoon, Dr. Jones.
       (one comma if the name is at the end of a sentence)
   Tell me, Bill, what did you think of the movie?
       (two commas around the name if it falls in the middle)

2. To float an interrupting phrase:

   I wanted to let you know, by the way, that you've just won a million dollars.

   The money is, however, not tax-free.

3. Before *and, but, or,* or *so* when two independent clauses are being joined:

   Othello thinks that he can trust Iago, but he is wrong.

Captain Ahab lost a leg to Moby-Dick, so he is seeking revenge.

Charlotte helps Wilbur believe in himself, and the pig wins first prize at the fair.

4.   Before quotation marks when dialogue is introduced by or followed by *said, remarked, cried,* and the like:

Jem said, "Yessum, she took us."

"Folks call me Cal," explained Calpurnia.

   Hint: P before Q (punctuation before quotation)

5.   In a series:

For the final exam you will need paper, a pen, a dictionary, and a brain.

I love to read The Phantom Tollbooth, Great Expectations, Moby-Dick, *and* Pride and Prejudice.

6.   In a complex sentence when the dependent clause comes first (see Chapter 5 for an explanation of complex sentences):

Whenever I brush my teeth before bed, my dreams smell sweet.

> *However confusing the rules on commas may be, they can be*
> *mastered with practice.*

The Echo Comma

Use a comma between two sentences that share the same *implied* verb. The following is not a run-on sentence:

> *Mr. Flippersnap sleeps until six A.M., Mrs. Flippersnap until*
> *noon.*

The verb *sleeps* is implied in the second half of the sentence, and since it is left out, we can join the halves with a comma. I call this kind of sentence echo writing, because the verb echoes from one part of the sentence to the next:

> *Mary had a little lamb, Sally a big fat one.*

> *My father drives a jalopy, my mother a Rolls-Royce.*

If echo writing feels comfortable, try to incorporate it into your own compositions; it will honor thy reader by making your sentences feel brisk.

Places You Might Be Tempted to Use a Comma but Shouldn't

1.   In a complex sentence when the dependent clause comes last:

WRONG: *My dreams smell sweet, whenever I brush my teeth before bed.*
RIGHT: *My dreams smell sweet whenever I brush my teeth before bed.*

2.   In a series when one of the items is a pair of Best Friend Nouns. Best Friend Nouns are nouns that normally go together:

Best Friend Nouns
(Don't let a comma come between them.)

salt and pepper
bread and butter
table and chairs
peanut butter and jelly
biscuits and gravy
rod and reel

WRONG: *When you set the table, be sure to remember the napkins, silverware, salt, and pepper.*
RIGHT: *When you set the table, be sure to remember the napkins, silverware, and salt and pepper.*

3.   Between subject and verb

WRONG: *Jack climbed the beanstalk, and stole gold from the giant.*
RIGHT: *Jack climbed the beanstalk and stole gold from the giant.*

WRONG: *Cinderella went to the ball, and danced with the prince.*
RIGHT: *Cinderella went to the ball and danced with the prince.*

Note: Experienced writers sometimes break this rule, and pause for effect.

4. By itself, between two sentences:

WRONG: *Goldilocks knocked on the Bears' door, they weren't home.*
RIGHT: *Goldilocks knocked on the Bears' door, but they weren't home.*
RIGHT: *Goldilocks knocked on the Bears' door; they weren't home.*

5. Between dissimilar adjectives:

WRONG: *We wore several, red sweaters.*
RIGHT: *We wore several red sweaters.*
RIGHT: *Clifford is a big, red dog. (Big and red are similar adjectives.)*

Hint: If you can switch the order, it's okay to slip in a comma:

Clifford is a red, big dog.

If you can't, leave the comma out:

Clifford has three young friends.
Clifford has young three friends.

6. Between the two parts of a compound noun:

WRONG: *We served a delightful brunch of eggs, bagels, orange, juice, and fruit.*

RIGHT:　*We served a delightful brunch of eggs, bagels, orange juice, and fruit.*

; (semicolon)

The semicolon seems to be an indecisive creature. If you turn it on its side, it looks like a confused face, half-smiling, half-sincere. In French they call it the *point-vergule,* which means "period-comma." (It's stronger than a comma but weaker than a period.) In English it's half a colon, which would be a serious medical condition if you had to digest your dinner with it. But in writing we don't use the semicolon to digest food; we use it to digest ideas.

A semicolon can join two sentences with a common theme:

> *In the morning I drink coffee with milk; in the evening I take it black.*

The theme of the two sentences—how I take my coffee—gives them something in common, a family tie almost. Just as you and your brother might like to share a room (when you're getting along), so the two like-themed sentences desire a closer tie than the period can provide.

> *The Rams were an unsuccessful football team in Los Angeles; in St. Louis they won the Super Bowl.*

The theme here is the success or failure of the Rams. The two sentences consider how well the team played in two different cities. We could separate them with a period:

> *The Rams were an unsuccessful football team in Los Angeles. In St. Louis they won the Super Bowl.*

The grammar here is fine, but the style feels choppy because the period brings us to a full stop when our mind wants to keep on rolling. The weaker stop of a semicolon makes a stronger tie between the two sentences and allows their contrast to sink right in.

You can also use a semicolon to link two sentences when the first one is the cause of the next:

> *I forgot to take a bath this morning; nobody wanted to sit beside me in class.*

> *Sam asked six different girls to the school dance; as a result, he left in an ambulance, and the girls became great friends.*

Those sentences could be separated by a period or by a comma and conjunction, but the semicolon speeds the reader's journey from setup to punch line. A good sentence, like a good joke, depends a lot on timing. When the first sentence causes a funny outcome in the next, the sooner your reader gets there, the better. Try linking them with a semicolon.

Like the center point of a teeter-totter, a semicolon is the fulcrum between two perfectly balanced sentences:

My aunt spent her New Year's Eve in Las Vegas; my uncle spent his in New York.

These two sentences show a contrast between my aunt's and my uncle's New Year's plans, yet their structure is in perfect harmony.

Jenny adores chocolate chip ice cream; Jason prefers pralines and cream.

The semicolon also keeps track of a long list that has commas within each item:

WRONG: *On my first trip to Europe, I visited London, England, Paris, France, Dublin, Ireland, and Rome, Italy.*

RIGHT: *On my first trip to Europe, I visited London, England; Paris, France; Dublin, Ireland; and Rome, Italy.*

Another handy use of the semicolon is to separate clauses that have commas within and a theme in common:

OKAY: *My dog is a canine of many talents. As a watchdog, she rattles our windows with her fierce barking. As a lapdog, she curls up into a tiny ball, warm and soft as a cashmere scarf. And as a retriever, she can find a tennis ball in a tangle of shrubs at the bottom of any canyon.*

BETTER: *My dog is a canine of many talents. As a watchdog, she rattles our windows with her fierce barking; as a lapdog, she curls up into a tiny ball, warm and soft as a cashmere scarf; and as a retriever, she can find a tennis ball in a tangle of shrubs at the bottom of any canyon.*

You could put the dog's talents in separate sentences (as in the first example), but since they are all connected by a common theme, it makes sense to let them hang together by a semicolon, which allows for a smoother ride.

: (colon)

Think of a colon as a pair of binoculars: it focuses the reader's eyes on something important. The sentence before the colon introduces the sentence or list that follows it.

> *It is important to be quiet in a library for one essential reason: too much noise distracts the characters.*

> *A good writer needs three basic skills: observation, concentration, and imagination.*

The launchpad of a colon should be a noun. Placing one after a preposition or a verb will make the reader dizzy.

WRONG: *I received e-mails today from: the Dalai Lama, the pope, and the president.*

RIGHT: *I received e-mails today from three old friends: the Dalai Lama, the pope, and the president.*

Colons introduce long or formal quotations:

In a confrontation with the Hogwarts bully Malfoy, Harry discovers his talent for handling a broomstick:

He mounted the broom and kicked hard against the ground and up, up he soared; air rushed through his hair, and his robes whipped out behind him—and in a rush of fierce joy he realized he'd found something he could do without being taught—this was easy, this was wonderful.

—Harry Potter and the Sorcerer's Stone

To keep certain information organized, use a colon:

1.   Between hours and minutes:

     2:45 P.M.
     9:00 A.M.

2.   Between chapter and verse of the Bible:

     Genesis 1:14
     Leviticus 3:12–15

3.   After the salutation in a formal letter:

     The Right Honorable Mr. McGoo:
     Dear President Scooby-Doo:
     To whom it may concern:

4. To separate a main title from its subtitle:

> *Poem-Making: Ways to Begin Writing Poetry* by Myra
>   Cohn Livingston
> *On Writing: A Memoir of the Craft* by Stephen King

— (dash)

What is the most challenging aspect of writing? Is it knowing where to start, how to end, or what to put in between? Is it getting an idea in the first place, or having to rewrite it a dozen times to get it right? For some writers the hardest part about writing isn't getting started or even finishing but maintaining a single train of thought.

Train of thought is a helpful metaphor for the writing process. A good piece of writing, like a train, carries the reader at a brisk pace along a track toward a clear destination. The only problem is that sometimes the writer gets distracted by the scenery along the way.

Not all detours are distractions. Sometimes when you are writing, a *relevant* thought will pop up and demand to be included. It could clarify your sentence or give a quick example or explanation. For these helpful intrusions our next mark of punctuation—the dash—was made.

As a verb, the word *dash* means "to move or act swiftly." If you *dash* off your homework on your way into class—and I catch you—I'll rip it up and make you do it over. If you *dash* off an essay at home—and I don't catch you—I'll probably find forty-seven Pen Commandment violations and make you do it over. If you *dash* out of the classroom before the bell rings—and I see you—I'll haul you back in and give you janitorial duty at recess.

But if you employ the dash in its noun form, I'm liable to commend you for experimenting with this useful and friendly mark of punctuation. I like the dash because it's the perfect example of how the human mind works. You don't have to have attention deficit disorder to have an active, multitasking brain. As you write, additional, modifying, or clarifying ideas will arrive unexpectedly, and the dash is ready to help you hand them off to your reader.

The "Aside" Dash

In the theater occasionally an actor will turn to the audience and comment on the scene onstage. In *Hamlet,* for example, Polonius comments on Hamlet's madness:

> HAM. . . . for yourself, sir, shall grow old as I am, if like
> a crab you could go backward.
>
> POL. [Aside.]   Though this be madness, yet
> there is method in't. Will you walk out of the
> air, my lord?
>
> HAM. Into my grave.
>
> POL. Indeed that is out of the air. [Aside.] How pregnant
> sometimes his replies are! (II.ii.193–211)

These asides are the dramatic equivalent of the dash. If a writer wants to break his sentence to make a side comment—I'm making one now—he uses a dash to set it off.

I did not remember our mother, but Jem did—he would tell me about her sometimes—and he went livid when Mrs. Dubose shot us this message.

—HARPER LEE,
To Kill a Mockingbird

Suddenly in the wood beyond The Water a flame leapt up—probably somebody lighting a wood fire—and he thought of plundering dragons settling on his quiet Hill and kindling it all to flames.

—J.R.R. TOLKIEN,
The Hobbit

The Defining Dash

You can also use a dash to give a quick definition of a word or phrase:

Part of a teacher's training today should include a crash course in online slang. A low-tech teacher who encounters "lol"—laugh out loud—in a student's paper might embarrass himself by marking the phrase as wrong.

The Example Dash

The dash is a handy tool for giving an example:

The most popular rides at Magic Mountain—Viper, Batman, and Superman—are best experienced before lunch, when crowds are thin and stomachs empty.

The topic for our most recent composition in English class was bizarre animal behaviors—a dog who licks his reflection in the mirror, a cat who watches television, a bird who sings the blues.

When the interrupting thought comes in the middle of the sentence, use two dashes to set it off; when it comes at the end, introduce it with a dash and end it with a period, a question mark, or an exclamation point.

The Emphatic Dash

At times you'll want to express something emphatically—that is, you want to drive it into the reader's mind for good. The versatile dash can help. In *Rascal,* Sterling North's memoir about his unforgettable childhood companion, the author recalls his sadness over the loss of his mother:

> *It seemed to me unfair that she could not have lived to see the pets I was raising—Rascal especially.*

Because Rascal is the star of Sterling's boyhood, he wants to single him out as the most important thing in his life that he would have liked to share with his mother. He makes this point by putting Rascal at the end of the sentence and introducing him with a dash.

J. K. Rowling uses the emphatic dash to build suspense in *Harry Potter and the Sorcerer's Stone:*

Harry leapt into the air; he'd trodden on something big and squashy on the doormat—something alive!

The Dialogue Dash

In life, people are always interrupting each other. Just listen to a classroom or schoolyard conversation, and you'll hear one person's speech cut off by another's.

"Hey, Mr. Frank, did you read my—"

"Here's my homework, Mr. Frank. I'm sorry it's—"

"Mr. Frank, could you read my poem and tell me if it's—"

"Hey, I was talking to him first."

In literature, characters often interrupt each other too. Watch as Milo gets the words snatched right out of this mouth in *The Phantom Tollbooth:*

"We're looking for a place to spend the night."

"It's not yours to spend," the bird shrieked again, and followed it with the same horrible laugh.

"That doesn't make any sense, you see—" he started to explain.

"Dollars or cents, it's still not yours to spend," the bird replied haughtily.

"But I didn't mean—" insisted Milo.

"Of course you're mean," interrupted the bird.

The Everpresent Wordsnatcher repeatedly interrupts Milo, and Norton Juster marks the rudeness with a dash.

If all the conversations in the world were punctuated the way they are written out on the page, there would be a barrage of flying dashes knocking everybody down—and knocking some politeness into us all. When your characters in a story are speaking, use the dash when one cuts another off. But when your friends are speaking, use a little courtesy and let them finish.

( ) (parentheses)

For a very brief interruption (and to vary the dash), try using parentheses. Parentheses are like drawers inside a sentence. They store incidental information, quick asides, and expressions:

> *Langston Hughes (1902–68) was a prominent poet of the Harlem Renaissance.*

> *We arrived late to the party (since there was an accident on the highway).*

> *On July 17, 1963, my mother gave birth to a (thank God) healthy baby boy.*

Punctuating sentences that contain parentheses can be tricky. But a little common sense clears things up. As a general rule, all punctuation goes outside the closing parenthesis:

WRONG: *We used to celebrate our birthdays at a restaurant called the Swiss Echo (which is out of business now.)*

RIGHT: *We used to celebrate our birthdays at a restaurant called the Swiss Echo (which is out of business now).*

The period belongs on the outside because it has to stop the whole sentence, not just the part in parentheses. But suppose the phrase inside your parentheses ends on a question mark or exclamation point. Then you have punctuate on the inside to avoid changing the meaning:

WRONG: *Anyone who has ever bought a lottery ticket (and who hasn't) knows that the chances of winning are slim.*

RIGHT: *Anyone who has ever bought a lottery ticket (and who hasn't?) knows that the chances of winning are slim.*

Sometimes, to give special emphasis, you'll write a stand-alone sentence and enclose it in parentheses. In this case, since the whole sentence is a parenthetical, put the period on the inside, as Anne Lamott does in this sentence from her excellent book on writing, *Bird by Bird*:

> *We were all so thrilled and proud, and this girl seemed to think I had the coolest possible father: a writer. (Her father sold cars.)*

When you aren't certain whether to use a dash or a pair of parentheses, follow this general rule: if it's something you want your reader to know right away—and it's worth interrupting the sentence for—use a dash; if it can wait until later (or you want a gentler break in the sentence), use parentheses.

- (hyphen)

A hyphen is like a joiner in a Hot Wheels set. Instead of connecting two pieces of track, it connects two or more words to make a compound:

mother-in-law	well-known
twenty-second	president-elect
self-restraint	knight-at-arms

Knowing when to hyphenate a compound can be tricky. Is it *dog-house* or *doghouse, back-pack* or *backpack, cross-eyed* or *crosseyed, fire fighter* or *fire-fighter?* Some compounds are written as two words; others are run together. There are so many rules about compounds—and so many exceptions to these rules—that it's best to consult a dictionary, as I did to discover it's *doghouse, backpack,* and *boardinghouse,* but *cross-eyed* and *firefighter* (no hyphen here).

The hyphen also holds on to parts of a word that must be broken at the end of a line. When you come to the end of a line in the middle of a word, be sure to divide it between syllables and double consonants or before the suffix, but never leave a single letter stranded:

WRONG:	hyp-hen	courage-ous
RIGHT:	hy-phen	coura-geous
WRONG:	profess-or	mocc-asin
RIGHT:	profes-sor	moc-casin

WRONG: a-bout   nois-y
RIGHT: about   noisy   (don't divide these)

' (apostrophe)

Being a teacher is like being a celebrity on a small scale. As captain of the classroom, you enjoy an instant mystique among the students. They observe you; they discuss you; they speculate about you. And sometime in the third week, when they're used to you, they start to ask questions.

"Mr. Frank, how'd you get that scar on your neck?"

"Mr. Frank, where'd you go to college?"

"Mr. Frank, are you married?"

"What's your first name, Mr. Frank?"

"How old are you?"

The truth about a first-year teacher is so scarce, he gets to invent it any way he wants.

"I got that scar saving a little kid from a coyote."

"I went to Cambridge University. I have two Ph.D.'s, one in astrophysics and the other in Renaissance literature. I've also got a black belt in kung fu."

"I'm not married, but it's against school policy for me to date your mom."

"My first name is Mister."

"I'm so old I can't remember my date of birth."

This last question—about my age—I haven't always answered so cleverly. Once I told a student, "I'm so old I used to play Pac-Man in the dorms at college."

"What's Pac-Man?"

"A video game where a little guy who looks like an apostrophe goes around eating dots."

"Never heard of it. You must be really old."

I *am* getting old if my video game references go back that far. (Actually, they go back to Pong.) Still, Pac-Man has a value that outlasts its primitive technology: it continues to be the perfect icon for when to use an apostrophe.

The apostrophe is a hungry little devil, like the Pac-Man guy (and his friend, Ms. Pac-Man). He has a strong appetite for condensing things, and so he goes around gobbling up expendable letters in order to make contractions. When Apostrophe Pac-Man sees *they are,* he gobbles up the *a* to make *they're.* When he sees *it is,* he swallows the second *i* and spits out *it's,* a swifter alternative for a more casual style. (Note: **Never** write *it's* for the possessive form; **always** spell it **its—no apostrophe**—as in *the dog devoured **its** bone.*) He gulps four letters to change *they would* to *they'd,* but his bottomless stomach never seems to be sated. *He will* becomes *he'll. Will not* becomes *won't. Have not* shrinks to *haven't.*

Apostrophe Pac-Man will never eat an *s,* though. To him, that would be the equivalent of cannibalism. He and the *s* are teammates, brothers almost, as they join forces to show possession.

To form the possessive of a singular noun, add *'s:*

The ark belongs to Noah. It's Noah's ark.
The wife of Sam is Allegra. Allegra is Sam's wife.

If the singular noun ends in *s*, you still add *'s*:

Charles's pen
Ross's girlfriend
Dickens's London

The only exceptions to this rule are the names *Moses* and *Jesus* or Greek names of more than one syllable ending in *s*. Moses' task, then, was to deliver the Ten Commandments, and Jesus' teachings were that we should follow them.

Plural nouns are less confusing. If they end in *s*, just add an apostrophe. If they don't end in *s*, add *'s*.

The dogs' barking kept us up for hours.
The Joneses' marriage lasted twenty-eight days.
The men's room is located next to the women's room.

The letter *s* is one of the most important letters of the alphabet. It begins some of my favorite names. But it has an even more important task that clearly makes it the most fertile consonant of the twenty-one: it forms plurals. The trouble is, some writers—and not only young ones—have developed a bad habit of throwing apostrophes at every *s* they see, just because they think the two always go hand in hand.

They don't.

An *s* (*es* after *X, ch, sh,* and *ss*) is sufficient to make a regular noun plural. The only time you should form a plural with *'s* is for symbols, abbreviations with periods in them, words-as-words, or letters-as-letters. In these cases it would be confusing to use the *s* alone:

CLEAR WITH S ALONE	NEEDS APOSTROPHE
In our AP English class, there were three 5s on the exam. The 1920s was a decade of decadence.	Six of our students went on to earn M.A.'s in literature. How many *x*'s are there in *Xerox*? Johnny was disappointed when he saw that his cuss words had been replaced by *'s, !'s, and $'s. Mr. Frank pointed out that I had used five *then*'s in one paragraph.

Sometimes Apostrophe Pac-Man gets so hungry, he can eat a century or more. Bill Clinton was elected president in 1992, but the date is often written as '92. Apostrophe Pac-Man gobbled up the 19. World War II lasted six years, from '39 to '45. The first man landed on the moon in '69, and somebody I know was born in '63.

The Apostrophe of Dialect

The apostrophe has always been the punctuation mark of dialect, or the speech patterns of a specific region. Mark Twain used it to capture the :Mississippi dialect of his characters in *The Adventures of Tom Sawyer*:

*"Oh, Tom, I reckon we're goners. I reckon there ain't no mistake
'bout where I'll go to. I been so wicked."*

*"Dad, fetch it! This comes of playing hookey and doing everything
a feller's told not to do. I might a been good, like Sid, if I'd a
tried—but not, I wouldn't, of course. But if ever I get off this
time, I lay I'll just waller in Sunday-schools!" And Tom began to
snuffle a little.*

*"You bad!" and Huckleberry began to snuffle too. "Consound it,
Tom Sawyer, you're just old pie, 'longside o' what I am."*

Charles Dickens used the apostrophe to render the particular speech patterns of the British working class. In *Great Expectations* the Convict ambushes Pip with, among other things, the
apostrophe of dialect: "Who d'ye live with—supposin' you're
kindly let to live, which I han't made up my mind about?" Joe
Gargery doesn't just drop his *g*'s; he drops his *h*'s too, referring to
Miss Havisham as "Miss 'Avisham." In *David Copperfield* Barkis is
"willin'," and Ham calls David "Mas'r Davy."

The first step to becoming a good writer is being a good
listener. Twain and Dickens heard their characters speaking,
but the power of their writing is that we can hear them too.
By dropping *g*'s, *h*'s, and even whole sections of words, they
used the apostrophe of dialect to preserve a piece of real life on
the page.

" " (quotation marks)

Quotation marks are shaped like ears. If they were therapists, their client schedules would be full. They'd make excellent parents, successful negotiators, fine watchdogs, and fair judges. They have the one quality essential for playing all of these roles: they're good listeners.

When you speak, words float out of your mouth escorted by quotation marks, which guide them from your lips to someone else's ears.

"Mr. Frank," I can hear you saying, "you're crazy. There aren't any quotation marks coming out of my mouth."

I say, "Look again. Go stand in front of a mirror and talk to yourself. Your spoken words will appear on the glass, surrounded by quotation marks."

Okay, fine. You didn't see them in the bathroom mirror. Then look in a book. Every time a character speaks, what do you see on either side of the dialogue? Quotation marks. Their purpose is to hold spoken words and to alert the reader to a change from narration to dialogue:

> *"What in the world ye fixin' to do, Jack?"*
> *"Well, Daddy," says Jack, "just as soon as I can find a place to ketch a hold, I'm a-goin' to take the creek back up there closer to the house to where your old woman can get her water everwhen she wants it."*

"Oh, no, Jack! Not take the creek back. Hit'll ruin my cornfield. And besides that, my old lady's gettin' sort-a shaky on her feet; she might fall in and get drownded."

—RICHARD CHASE,
The Jack Tales

Notice how the author has enclosed the exact spoken words of the characters in quotation marks. Notice also that the dialogue is introduced by a comma so that the reader will be alerted to a change in speaker. In your own writing, remember to put your P (punctuation) before Q (quotation)—unless, that is, your P changes the meaning of your Q:

WRONG: *Joe said "I see the stars winking at night".*
RIGHT: *Joe said, "I see the stars winking at night."*

The comma introducing Joe's quote comes before the quotation mark, as does the period ending it. But if a punctuation mark would change the meaning of the sentence, then it belongs *outside* the quotation marks.

WRONG: *Did Joe say, "I see the stars winking at night?"*
RIGHT: *Did Joe say, "I see the stars winking at night"?*

When it comes to titles, use quotation marks around titles that don't weigh too much, such as those for short stories, poems, newspaper and magazine articles, and songs. Heavier items such as books, magazines, and newspapers need something stronger to support them. For these titles we use the underline, which acts like a shelf to hold them up, or *italics,* which shoulders them:

| *Quoted Titles* | *Underlined Titles* |
| | *(or in italics)* |

"The Lottery" by Shirley Jackson	<u>Moby-Dick</u> by Melville (or *Moby-Dick*)
"Imagine" by John Lennon	<u>The Encyclopedia of American Music</u>
"Why Johnny Can't Read"	<u>Time</u>

Quotation marks don't like to be crowded. Every time you change speakers, you should change paragraphs too:

WRONG: *"Unhand that damsel in distress!" commanded Quixote. "Make me, you cardboard-wearing, half-dead horse-riding, long-word-using wimp!" said the salesman, clutching a life-sized Julia Roberts doll.*

RIGHT: *"Unhand that damsel in distress!" commanded Quixote.*
    "Make me, you cardboard-wearing, half-dead horse-riding, long-word-using wimp!" said the salesman, clutching a life-sized Julia Roberts doll.

—FROM A STUDENT'S STORY ABOUT DON QUIXOTE
IN OUR TIME

Giving each new speaker his or her own paragraph is a nice way to share the stage. We all like to be heard when we speak, and our characters are no different. A new paragraph signals the reader that you are moving on to a new speaker. That way nobody gets ignored.

? (question mark)

Tall, curvaceous, curious, the question mark ends a sentence in the most provocative way possible: by forming a question.

Even her shape is whimsical. Curling up from a period like a genie from its bottle, she hovers slightly above the line, a balloon just beyond our reach. Unlike the genie, though, she doesn't grant our wishes; instead, she piques our curiosity, lures us into a *quest* for knowledge.

Socrates understood the power of a question. Instead of telling his students information, he would ask them a series of questions and coax them into thinking for themselves. His students felt either very stupid (if they never got the right answer) or very smug (if they often did). I've always thought the Socratic method works best when there is no right answer, just a series of questions that lead to more questions like doors in a maze. The point isn't how much you know but how much you *want* to know. Ask yourself, *What if? How? Who? When? Where? Why?* And watch where the questions take you.

Human progress is the result of asking questions. Copernicus asked questions about the night sky and concluded that human beings aren't the center of the universe after all. Newton wondered why an apple clunked him on the head and discovered that gravity was weighing it down. Darwin pondered the differences among finches from one Galápagos island to the next; his questions led to the theory of evolution. And the questions Bill Gates asked about how people might use a personal computer led to the word-processing program I'm using right now. From Socrates to Microsoft, the question mark has led the way.

Down with Up-talk!

In recent years there has been a tendency to overuse the question mark, especially in speech. It's as though a large portion of the human population had swallowed a bar of soap in the shape of a question mark, so that when we speak, tiny interrogative bubbles come floating out of our mouths after everything we say. This phenomenon, known as up-talk, is one of the most widespread speech impediments of our time, and it's causing the question mark to have a nervous breakdown.

Question marks belong at the end of a question, not a statement? It's like, you know, they really weren't designed to be used so much? I mean, we're killing their mystery? And worse, we're making ourselves seem all unsure? Up-talk is, like, what little kids do when they're trying to get a grown-up's attention? To see if the grown-up is listening? But it's better to get someone's attention by being bold and confident instead of all tentative?

Up-talk puts you down. If everything you say sounds like a question, who's going to take you seriously? A question mark at the end of a command makes it a plea, at the end of an emotion makes it a pity, and at the end of an idea makes it a dud. Imagine a policeman shouting after a gunman, "Stop or I'll shoot?"

Imagine Jonas Salk addressing the World Health Organization by saying, "I've found a vaccine? For polio?" And imagine yourself turning to your boyfriend or girlfriend after a particularly romantic evening and saying, "I love you?"

It's likely to be your last date.

! (exclamation point)

Cut out all those exclamation marks. An exclamation mark is like laughing at your own joke.

——F. SCOTT FITZGERALD

Do you know any people who are just a little bit loud? It could be that they're feeling up when you're feeling down, or that they have a constant flow of caffeine in their bloodstream, or that nobody listens to them so they feel compelled to shout. We've all encountered these eardrum-beaters at one time or another. We wince, or we flee, or we plug our ears. Sometimes, out of politeness, we listen and nod. Most of the time we find ourselves wishing for a magic remote control that would mute them.

The exclamation point is like these high-decibel people. Tall, strident, and stiff, it lacks the elegance of the question mark or the confidence of the period. Tentative writers use it to hide their fear, lazy ones to create the missing emotion in a sentence. Greeting card writers use it on Valentine's Day to declare, "I LOVE YOU!!!!!" Department stores use it on signs announcing a SALE!!!

While an undergrad at UC Berkeley, I used to walk through Sproul Plaza with a friend I'll call Phil. Phil was always bursting with nervous energy and enthusiasm, like a windup toy that never winds down. I used to enjoy walking with him early in the morning because his presence was a jolt of electricity that helped wake me for my nine o'clock class.

At the same time Phil was an embarrassment. Exclamation points flew out of his mouth like arrows. Their target was usually someone he wanted to impress, one of his teachers or a girl in his dorm. "Hey, Professor! Great lecture yesterday! I'll see you at office hours!" The dazed and blinking professor would look around, but he would have needed binoculars to bridge the gap of three hundred yards from Phil's mouth to his own ear.

"Vanessa! Over here! It's me, Phil!" The attractive but discreet Vanessa would try to dodge the dart, but Phil would just increase the volume of his attack. "You look terrific today!!!"

After ten minutes of Phil's cross-campus salutations, I would be wide awake. The only trouble was that by the time I sat down to hear a lecture, I was completely deaf. Phil and his exclamation points became too much for me, so to get myself going in the morning, I switched from his company to a cappuccino. Don't get me wrong. I like enthusiasm—in moderation. In writing, as in speaking, the exclamation point is best used sparingly and in the right context.

It is most appropriate in dialogue. If a fire breaks out in a story you're writing, by all means have a character shout, "FIRE!" If someone is moved by the sight of fresh snow on a red barn, you can express his awe with an exclamation point:

"Look at that!" If your protagonist wins the lottery, "Hooray *period*" is a bit tame. Let her erupt, "Hooray!" But no matter how much she won, a single exclamation point will do. Leave the doubles and the triples to the managers at Macy's.

A good rule of thumb is that the exclamation point is the written equivalent of passion. Where you would raise your voice, raise an exclamation mark. But if you can be persuasive, romantic, enthusiastic, or upset without yelling, then let your words speak for themselves.

Now that we've learned to stop picking on the Puncts, I think we can avert a strike. After all . . .

A punctuation strike would be worse than an air traffic controllers' strike, a janitors' strike, and a nurses' strike combined. Imagine if all our sentences were unmarked and all our thoughts allowed to spill willy-nilly onto the page. How would you know when one sentence ended and the next began? How would your reader be able to find—let alone board—your train of thought? Our sentences would no longer communicate; they would confuse. The result: a meltdown in communication, a nervous breakdown among all human beings. Meanwhile, the eleven marks of punctuation (twelve if you count the ellipsis) would be picketing in the margins of our newspapers, books, and essays: "Puncts on strike! Puncts on strike!" What a sad day for humanity!

Five

Thou Shalt Keep Thy Structure Holy

AS THE YOUNGEST OF THREE SONS, I spent much of my childhood yearning for privileges ahead of time. My older brothers got to stay up later, cross the street sooner, eat larger portions of dessert, and ride bikes without training wheels long before I ever could.

This last privilege, of riding a big-kid bike, was one I coveted so much that I found a way to get it early. My father had an impressive and well-organized collection of tools in the garage, each one hanging from a pegboard and outlined in black ink so that you'd remember exactly where it went. One day just before I turned five, I used a rake to bump his hammer off its peg and onto the ground. Then I carried it into the breezeway, where my bicycle stood upright and perfectly straight on a pair of training wheels.

For the next ten minutes, I unleashed all my rage at being the last to stay up late, the last to cross the street without holding a grown-up's hand, and the last to size my own piece of cake. I pummeled and clawed and scraped and smashed those training wheels until they looked like they'd been run over by a garbage truck.

When my father came home from work that day, I was sitting on the front steps, my head held in my hands, crying made-up tears.

"What's the matter?" my dad asked.

"I bumped into the steps," I said. "My bike's ruined."

He went over and inspected the damage. "You must have been riding very fast."

"No," I said. "I was riding along at a safe speed. But these steps are made of brick, and they can do a lot of damage."

"Well, looks like we'll have to get you a new set of training wheels."

"Yeah—unless you want to just take those ones off."

"Aren't you a little young to be riding a straight two-wheeler?"

"Not if you teach me," I said hopefully.

His head bounced around a bit as he considered. "All right, we'll take 'em off," he said. "I'll go get the pliers."

Moments later my father returned with a pair of pliers in his hand and a smile on his face. "So you hit the step, huh?" he asked, loosening the nut.

"Yeah. I misjudged how wide the training wheels were."

He nodded and unclamped the training wheels, which he tossed in a heap to one side. Then he turned to me and said, "Hop on."

For the next half-hour, with daylight fading, my father

taught me how to write a two-wheeler all by myself. He ran alongside me, holding the bike upright and urging me to "pedal ... faster ... faster" as I struggled to get up enough speed not to fall. But I fell. Over and over again, he set me back on the seat, accompanied me on a running start, and then let go. And over and over I pumped those pedals, but not long enough or fast enough to keep my balance.

When I saw him eyeing my dead training wheels on the grass, I sensed his frustration and said, "Come on, Dad. This time I think I can get it." I climbed back on. He counted one-two-three ... and then he ran with me as I started to pedal. This time, when he let go, I kept pedaling. And this time I didn't fall. I rode that two-wheeler right through the breezeway, onto the driveway, and across the street, claiming two privileges before my time and both in a single day.

Afterward my father said he was proud of me for not giving up. He offered to throw the training wheels into the trash and asked me to put the pliers back. I picked them up and headed into the garage. Reaching up to hang the pliers on their outlined spot, I noticed, up above, the empty outline of a capital *T*. And beneath the pliers, sharing pegs with a hand shovel, was the hammer I'd put back in the wrong place.

To this day I don't know whether my father saw the empty spot on the pegboard. I don't know if he realized that the training wheels didn't collide with the front steps but with his hammer being swung by a youngest son impatient to grow up. But the following Thursday, when our trash was taken away, so were my training wheels. And the next time I went into the garage, the hammer was back on its own peg.

I tell this story of my assault on training wheels because I'm about to offer you set of training wheels for the compositions you write. In this chapter we'll take a look at structure in general and see how it applies to writing. In the next chapter we'll look at some typical essay topics and how best to tackle them. I'll include sample compositions and outlines to guide you. Use the outlines if they're helpful, if they keep your writing on course and your thoughts in focus. Use them if you get stuck and need a jump start. And when you're ready to write without them, grab a hammer and have some fun.

A sentence expresses a single thought. A paragraph expresses a single idea. A composition expresses a single big idea. A book contains many big ideas, all of which add up to an even bigger idea. A library contains most of the big ideas human beings have ever had (and published). The Library of Congress contains them all. The Internet contains every worthless and worthwhile idea a human being has ever posted on a website.

What do all of these forms of expression have in common? Structure. Structure is the pattern that keeps things from falling apart—or down. Human beings have perfect structure: a skeleton that holds us together—and up. Our cells have structure too: a nucleus, or center, and a cytoplasm to surround, protect, and feed that nucleus. These cells join with other cells to create the structure for our bones, organs, bile, and blood. Our bodies and brains have enabled us to create other structures, from Stonehenge to the Golden Gate Bridge, from the chariot to the Model T, from the typewriter to the Palm Pilot. This building where I'm working, for instance—the library at my school—has a solid foundation, support columns, and dozens of floor joists to prevent me from landing on my southern cheeks two stories down. Its structure is probably similar to the Lego towers or tree houses you built as a kid, and to the extraordinary cathedrals built during the Middle Ages and Renaissance in homage to God.

It's easy to identify the structure of a building, a chair, or a cell. It's easy to spot the structure of a tree, a bridge, or a boat. The structure of the United States government is precisely mapped out by the Constitution. The pattern of a sonata or symphony is readily apparent to a well-trained ear. The structure of a paragraph, poem, composition, or novel, however, is abstract and therefore harder to see.

But it's there. And no matter how invisible it may seem, it's essential to good writing.

What Is a Topic Sentence?

A paragraph is like a room, not yours or mine—they're too messy—but a room with a clear purpose: everything inside serves a main idea. And before we let a reader enter the room of our paragraph, we hang a sign on the door: the topic sentence.

The topic sentence is your contract with the reader. It states what the paragraph will be about and promises that you will stick to that main idea. Read the following topic sentence for a paragraph of comparison:

My goldfish and my uncle have many things in common.

This topic sentence promises that the paragraph will explain how your uncle and your goldfish are alike. Each supporting sentence has to help fulfill that promise, or else the reader will get lost:

One similarity between the two is their passion for water. My goldfish delights in swimming all day, and my uncle seldom misses his afternoon dip in the pool. My uncle and my goldfish also share the same temperament. Both are quiet and somewhat shy. You could say that by nature they are observers more than participants: they even have the same bulging eyes that follow me whenever I walk past. They have other similar features too. I won my goldfish in a raffle at the school fair. The scales on my goldfish's back are the identical shade of orange as the hairs on my uncle's chest. And my uncle's habit of rubbing body oil on his arms and legs makes his skin as iridescent as my fish's scales. Another similarity between my fish and my uncle is their taste in food. My goldfish loves the fish flakes I pour in his tank twice a day, just as my uncle adores the cornflakes that my aunt pours in his bowl. In fact, though they both like to swim, each could benefit from swimming a bit faster, as their plump bellies would suggest. Of all their similarities, the thing my uncle and my goldfish most have in common is that they both enjoy a visit from me.

One of the sentences in the paragraph strays from the topic sentence. It provides information that has absolutely nothing to do with the comparison between the uncle and the fish. Can you find this stowaway sentence and kick it out?

If you chose the sentence about cornflakes and fish flakes, you must not like cereal very much. If you chose the one about winning the goldfish at the school fair, good for you. While this sentence may contain an interesting fact, it has nothing to do with the main idea of the paragraph—the similarities between the uncle and the fish. Now, if my aunt had won my uncle in, say, a poker game, then my winning the fish in the raffle would be a relevant point: both would have been booty. But she didn't. They met as young screenwriters at MGM, when he bribed a fellow writer fifty-dollars to get the office next to hers.

Does the Topic Sentence Have to Come First?

My brother Dan and I used to play a terrifying game called Hide and Scare. One of us would hide, and the other would count down from fifty. At zero the seeker would creep through the empty and often dark house, chanting, "A-boo a-boo a-boo a-boo a-boo a-boo a-boooooo" to the tune of *The Pink Panther*. He would creak open doors to bedrooms, closets, and bathrooms, knowing that at any moment the other guy would JUMP OUT AND SCARE him. Then we'd time how long it took for the seeker's heart rate to return to normal. Whoever caused a heart to race longer won.

Hide and Scare offers the same kind of thrill as a haunted mansion or a horror film: the wallop of surprise. If every room in our house had a sign on it announcing YES, HE'S IN HERE or NO, HE'S NOT, the game wouldn't be much fun. Similarly, if every paragraph you write places its topic sentence up front, your writing will tend to be predictable, and your reader's heart will never race.

Read the following paragraph about child laborers in the early 1900s. Notice where the topic sentence falls:

> *Thousands of young boys descended into dark and dangerous coal mines every day, or worked aboveground in the stifling dust of the coal breakers, picking slate from coal with torn bleeding fingers. Small girls tended noisy machines in the spinning rooms of cotton mills, where the humid, lint-filled air made breathing difficult. They were kept awake by having cold water thrown in their faces. Three-year-olds could be found in the cotton fields, twelve-year-olds on factory night shifts. Across the country, children who should have been in school or at play had to work for a living.*
>
> —RUSSELL FREEDMAN,
> *Kids at Work: Lewis Hine and*
> *the Crusade Against Child Labor*

The main idea is not stated up front; it unfolds as you read and is made clear only in the last sentence, a summarizing farewell that is topic sentence and conclusion both in one.

How Do I Write a Concluding Sentence?

Conclusions are a challenge to write. I can easily teach students how to write a topic sentence and how to organize their supporting sentences in a logical way. I can advise them to come up with at least three strong points to serve the main idea and to give each point a few sentences of support. I can tell them that it's a good strategy to save the best point for last and to make sure that no irrelevant details sneak into their paragraph. But students often ask what they should write in the conclusion. And my answer is "That depends."

Your conclusion depends on everything *specific* that comes before it. Each paragraph or composition or report or short story or poem or book that you write will suggest its own conclusion, but not before you start writing it. Here I am on page 118 of *The Pen Commandments,* and I'm still not certain what my conclusion will be. Some writers do know the ending of their novel or play before they write the beginning, but in most cases the ending comes later, after the writer has spent time developing a story and becoming better friends with the characters. For the purpose of teaching structure, I can say that the conclusion belongs at the end and that it should leave the reader with an afterthought, a tiny twist to what has preceded it. A good conclusion takes the topic sentence and tosses it like a stone into a lake, causing ripples in the reader's mind. If the reaction you get to your conclusion is a smile or a laugh or a "Hmmmm" or even a "Wow!" you know you've written a good one.

Read the following paragraph about a family ritual. The conclusion didn't suggest itself until I got to the end.

TOPIC: WRITE A PARAGRAPH
ABOUT A FAMILY RITUAL

To the Rocks

Our family is scattered across the country, but every August we come together on the shore of the Pacific

Northwest coast, and we begin our reunion with a walk to the rocks. From New York, Los Angeles, and Seattle, the usually distant ends of the family share a narrow path from Grandma and Grandpa's summer home through the dunes and onto the beach. Because the path has been untouched for twelve months, it is overgrown with dune grass, wildflowers, and branches from untrimmed trees. My father, who at seventy-five still wields a scythe like Lewis and Clark, leads the way. He is followed by his three sons and five grandchildren. The wives and Grandma bring up the rear. (They prefer gossiping to clearing ground.) Once the colony reaches the shore, we fan out in a new formation, like the flock of sandpipers scurrying out of our way. In the distance a beacon of light declares our destination: the rocks at the foot of North Head lighthouse. For the next thirty minutes we walk into the wind, raising our voices above the churn and spray of a turbulent sea. A year's worth of milestones get reviewed. Secrets are shared, old wounds are reopened, apologies are sometimes made. By the time our twenty-two hands touch the jagged, slippery rocks, we may not all be getting along, but we are getting closer, and we still have the walk home.

When asked to explain his writing process, James Joyce said, "I am like a man who stumbles along. My foot strikes something. I bend down and pick it up. And it is *exactly* what I want." We can't all be as lucky as James Joyce, but we can heed the good advice his comment implies, particularly about writing a conclusion: let it come. If you are too self-conscious, too fixated on what your conclusion will be, it won't feel like a natural, inevitable by-product of everything leading up to it. In the paragraph above, the conclusion I stumbled upon was to suggest that although the walk to the rocks doesn't resolve all the conflicts it may raise, the family still has the walk home to continue the reunion. I didn't plan it this way, but it ended up literally reversing the topic sentence and offering the reader an optimistic hint of things to come.

The only rule for a conclusion is that it has to wrap things up or suggest the need for further thought. It's the sign on the *inside* of the front door, and it makes it okay for the reader to leave.

When Do I Change Paragraphs?

You start a new paragraph each time you start a new main idea. Suppose you were asked to compare *and* contrast two members of your family. If you chose your fish and your uncle, and you'd written one paragraph on their similarities, you would start a new one to explain their differences:

> *Although they have many things in common, my uncle and my goldfish do have a few significant differences.*

This new topic sentence signals a change in main ideas. George Schoenman, my high school English teacher, called it "a transitional topic sentence" because it shifts the reader's attention from one category (similarities) to the next (differences). If you don't bother to start a new paragraph, you'll be cramming two main ideas into one space, and the room will be a mess.

You should also change paragraphs to signal a change in time or place. Which of the following versions from James Reeves's translation of *Don Quixote* do you think is easier to read?

1. "All I need," said Quixote, "is rest and food. Get me something to eat, good woman, and let me go to bed to repose my weary limbs after my adventures and hardships." So Quixote went off to bed, and when she had seen to his needs the housekeeper went to the library to help the priest and the barber carry his books out to the courtyard. In the morning, before Quixote was awake, a great bonfire was made on the stones, and all those mischievous books of knighthood and romance were burnt to ashes. Some few, which were less harmful than the rest, and which were thought to be valuable, were saved; but the greater part of them went up in flames, never again to be read by the eyes of man. Thus did Quixote's friends think they had cured him of his madness.

2. "All I need," said Quixote, "is rest and food. Get me something to eat, good woman, and let me go to bed to repose my weary limbs after my adventures and hardships."

So Quixote went off to bed, and when she had seen to his needs the housekeeper went to the library to help the priest and the barber carry his books out to the courtyard.

In the morning, before Quixote was awake, a great bonfire was made on the stones, and all those mischievous books of knighthood and romance were burnt to ashes. Some few, which were less harmful than the rest, and which were thought to be valuable, were saved; but the greater part of them went up in flames, never again to be read by the eyes of man. Thus did Quixote's friends think they had cured him of his madness.

Version 1 jams all the information into one overcrowded paragraph; 2 logically arranges the same information into three separate paragraphs. The first break shows a change in place—Quixote goes off to bed. The second shows a break in time—it takes us into the next morning. When you read the two versions side by side like this, it is easy to see how paragraph divisions make sense. But in the rush of writing, especially when the composition is due in less than twenty minutes, your paragraphs tend to run together. Just as you clean up your room before a friend comes over, be sure to clean up your paragraphs before you invite a reader in.

"Finally, remember to start a new paragraph when you change speakers in dialogue," Mr. Frank said to his class.

"Why?" one student asked.

"To help the reader keep track of who's talking."

"Why can't I just open and close quotation marks? Changing paragraphs wastes time and paper."

"But it saves words. I don't have to write *said Mr. Frank* after this piece of dialogue, because I changed paragraphs. My reader intuits the change of speaker."

"How will I remember the rule?"

"Easy. Pretend all your dialogue gets delivered over a two-way radio. With walkie-talkies, when one speaker finishes talking, he says *over* and then waits for the other to speak. In writing, that *over* is expressed visually, in the form of a new paragraph."

"I'll remember that, Mr. Frank. Over."

"Over and out."

It's Too Crowded in Here: Writing a Multiparagraph Composition

When I moved into an eleven-hundred-square-foot apartment on North Kings Road, I felt like royalty. It was the first time I'd lived all alone, the first time I had my own kitchen, dining room, living room, bathroom, and empty closets. I turned the dining room into a large office and pitched my desk smack in the center, with the chair facing out so I could preside like an executive. I stayed up obscenely late, watching old movies, reading books, and writing. There was a fireplace in the living room, and on its mantel sat my collection of old typewriters, from a 1920 Corona to the first electric typewriter ever made. Each night I'd take a different typewriter to bed with me. There we'd spend a little quality time writing in my journal before I fell asleep.

Then I got engaged. The fiancée moved in. The closets filled up. The office turned back into a dining room, and I stopped taking my typewriters to bed.

Two years after we were married, a third roommate moved in—a beautiful baby girl. The dining room became the baby's room, and our daughter became the first kid with a chandelier over her crib. There is an old Spanish expression that goes,

"Baby brings the bread," meaning that when a baby comes, she brings good fortune with her. I don't know what the Spanish word for *clutter* is, but she brought a lot of that too. Before long my palace on North Kings Road was looking like a preschool.

There were two solutions to this problem: (1) give the daughter up for adoption, toys included, and divorce the wife, wedding gifts included; or (2) build a house. I opted for the second choice. We're still planning and saving for that new house, and our apartment is getting more and more crowded, but I think I made the right choice. Staying in that one-bedroom apartment would be like living in a one-paragraph composition for the rest of my life. I want to experience—and express—more.

In writing, if you can't fit everything you want to say into a single paragraph, you should build yourself a house. A writer's land is cheap (all you need is paper), but the multiparagraph composition you build, like a house, needs to have a solid foundation and a set of plans.

You should start with a thesis sentence. A thesis sentence is a kind of topic sentence, only instead of setting up one paragraph, it sets up many. Suppose you are writing an essay entitled "My Father's First Car." You are asked to interview your dad and develop his answers into a composition. It's a good idea to settle on a thesis sentence before structuring the essay. Which of the following thesis sentences would you choose to welcome your reader?

1. My father kept a scarf in the glove compartment of his 1948 Buick convertible.

2. On his seventeenth birthday, my father bought himself a present, a 1948 Buick convertible—his first car.

3. A 1948 Buick convertible got ten miles to the gallon of gasoline and demanded thirty-seven cents for a full tank.

4. When I turn eighteen, I'm going to buy myself an electric car.

Choice 1 is too specific to be the sign on the door but would make a good support sentence for inside. Choice 3, too, sounds like a supporting detail and would confuse the reader if it were his first contact with your essay. Choice 4 clearly reflects your environmentally conscious intentions but has absolutely nothing to do with the topic. Choice 2, however, is a good and vivid thesis sentence, because it focuses the reader's attention on your father's first car.

The Introduction: The Steps to the Front Door

Students have a lot of anxiety about length. I don't give assignments that have a minimum number of words, lines, or pages. When I'm asked, "How long does it have to be?" I answer, "As long as it takes for you to feel proud of your work." This cagey response sometimes frustrates students who have been programmed to fill a specific number of pages, but it also frees them to be more creative in both the substance of what they write and in its structure.

A multiparagraph composition seems like a daunting task, but in many ways it is easier to write than a single paragraph. For one thing, it allows you to develop more sophisticated thoughts than can be conveyed in a single paragraph. For another, it gives you the freedom to grab the reader's attention in your very own way. And the place to hook the reader is in the introduction.

Instead of a single topic sentence, you get to write a whole paragraph that begins or ends with the thesis statement. George Schoenman taught us to make the thesis statement the last sentence of the introduction. He had a side job as head usher at Dodger Stadium, and he liked to use baseball metaphors in his teaching. "When you write an introduction," he told us, "start somewhere in left field and then work your way to home plate, which is your thesis statement." Another teacher at my high school agreed that the thesis statement should come last, but she had worked as a bartender in her twenties and used a different metaphor: "Your introduction is a martini glass—it starts with a wide cup and then narrows to form the thesis statement." My brother once had an English teacher whose hobby was hunting. This man thought the thesis statement should come first. "Start your introduction with a bang," he said. "Put your thesis statement up front, and make it as good as a gunshot in the forest. Once you've turned your reader's head, you can lure him in, and the hunt is on."

I'm still partial to the house metaphor. The composition is your house; the supporting paragraphs are rooms inside the house; and the introduction is the walkway leading to the front door, where the thesis statement hangs like a welcome sign. Or if you like your thesis to come first, it's a balloon tied to the mailbox. Choose any of these metaphors—or better yet, come up with one of your own. It doesn't really matter which you prefer, as long as your introduction grabs your reader's attention and lets her know what your essay will be about.

There are many ways to start an introduction. You could offer a quote and show how it relates to your thesis. You could begin with an anecdote, a brief story that sets up your thesis. You could cite some statistics that might surprise the reader and pique his curiosity. You could start by posing a question. Or you could make an outrageous statement designed to shock your reader.

If I were writing about my father's first car, I'd try to craft an introduction that establishes a humorous tone and ends with a surprise:

> On his seventeenth birthday, my father bought himself a present, a 1948 Buick convertible—his first car. This lavish gift he purchased with the collective earnings from six odd jobs—paperboy, bowling alley pinsetter, lawn mower, baby-sitter, lemonade-stand proprietor, and fence painter—along with a sizable loan from his grandmother.

It's a brief introduction, just two sentences long. It takes the hunter's approach, placing the thesis statement up front, then puts a humorous twist on the thesis by revealing that the grandma paid for most of the car.

Support Paragraphs: Each One a Room in Your Home

Now that we have an introduction, how do we build the inside of our house? Depending on how talkative your dad is in the interview, you'll probably get several interesting facts about his first car, and it's up to you to organize them in a logical way. Maybe you start with a description of the car—color, size, shape, type of seats. Then you can move on to the engine—cylinders, horsepower, gas mileage. More interesting, of course, would be to write about the *outings* your father and his 1948 Buick went on—road trips, rides, and dates. How did his life change when he got it? Did he ever dent the fender? Forget where he parked? Get in a chase?

If you begin with a description of the car, make sure you honor thy reader by making it memorable. Rather than just listing the facts of color, shape, and size, try to think of a *context,* or situation, that makes the description more vivid:

> My father's relationship with his 1948 Buick began as love at first sight. One rainy November afternoon while taking the trolley home from school, he passed the window of a Buick dealer in downtown Portland. When his eye caught the sleek yellow hood, gleaming whitewall tires, and seaworthy fins of the latest convertible, my father leaped off the moving trolley and splashed through puddles to get a closer look.

Love at first sight fits well as a metaphor for a teenager's infatuation with a car. It also gives us a little detail to plant here and pay off later. To finish the beat and bring forward something mentioned in the introduction, you could include a sentence about how his grandma got involved:

> Every day for six weeks he visited his beloved Buick, and on the day before his seventeenth birthday, he introduced her to his grandmother, who approved of the match.

The next logical step would be a paragraph about how the new car changed your father's life.

> With his hand on the steering wheel and his name on the registration, my father felt like a city slicker, a cool cat, a man about town. But with his grandmother in the passenger seat, he felt more like a chauffeur. After one hundred and five rides to the Rotary Club, the market, and the cemetery to visit Grandpa, his grandmother announced that the loan had officially been repaid, and he was free to give rides to girls his own age.

Since you've mentioned dating, you can introduce a memorable detail from the interview: the scarf he kept in the glove compartment.

> Now that he could expect passengers with longer hair, my father bought the first accessory for his Buick—a blue-and-white silk scarf, which he kept neatly folded

in the glove compartment. The scarf embraced many heads in its day, as my father developed a reputation for gallantry along with his good looks.

Here it might make sense to include a quote from the interview. Quotes lend variety to an essay by breaking up the pattern and bringing a new voice to the reader's ear.

"The Buick gave me independence, confidence, charisma," he explained. "Asking a girl to take the trolley with you to see a movie is one thing, but taking her to a drive-in in your Buick is a whole other ball of wax. You can't pull over and park when you're on the trolley."

At this point you could tell the story of the first time your dad crashed his new car.

In the ten years that my father drove his '48 Buick, he got in only one accident. He was cruising along Broadway in downtown Portland when something caught his eye. That something was the long leg of a woman stepping out of Meier & Frank's department store. It was such a beautiful leg, and belonged to such a beautiful woman, that it caused my father to rear-end the delivery truck parked in front of him. This second case of love at first sight put a huge dent in the first. The woman looked over, saw that he'd been admiring her, and smiled. She was wearing a bright green silk scarf, and in time it replaced the blue-and-white one in the glove compartment of the Buick. It's really a lovely scarf—my mother still wears it on a windy day.

Now that I reread that one paragraph, I see it should be broken into two. The question is, where to break it? The first part is about the accident, the second about the aftermath. Since the look between my father and mother is more intimate than the crash, it feels like *The woman looked over* should begin its own paragraph. And since it includes the twist of that long-legged lady turning out to be the author's mom, it feels like a natural way to conclude.

I've just taken you through the process of writing this composition. My approach is to plan and write at the same time. But I could have just as effectively done the planning first, in an outline. An outline is the blueprint for your essay: it can be a highly detailed list of steps or a brief sketch:

I. Introduction and thesis sentence—Dad bought himself car for seventeenth birthday
Odd jobs. Loan from Grandma

II. Love at first sight
A. Car caught his eye
B. Ran through rain for closer look
C. Brought Grandma to see—she approved

III. Changed life
A. Felt like a man
B. Except with Grandma as passenger
C. Loan "repaid"

IV. Began to date
    A. Bought scarf
    B. Quote: took girls to drive-ins

V. The accident
    A. Saw woman step out of department store
    B. Rear-ended delivery truck
    C. Second love at first sight damaged first

VI. Conclusion—Lady was my mom

Whether you do a detailed outline or a brief sketch doesn't really matter. What matters is that you think deeply about your topic and end up with a logical, well-structured essay.

Transition Words and Sentences: So the Reader Won't Get Lost

A one-paragraph essay with a clear topic sentence and several points of support is easy for a reader to follow. A multi-paragraph composition, on the other hand, needs to have a clearly marked path. Once we've got our reader inside our house, we keep him from getting lost by holding his hand. And the way we hold his hand is by using transition words.

Transition means passage from one place, phase, or idea to another. Transition words and phrases are like hallways in a house—they alert the reader every time we shift our thoughts. This could be a shift in time, location, or importance. It could move from one idea to another, showing how they are similar or different. It could even indicate a shift from a cause to its effect.

If I were writing a multiparagraph composition about three un forgettable neighbors, I would want to preserve each in a paragraph of his or her own. I would begin with some introductory thoughts on neighbors in general—how they are the unpredictable part of the scenery around you: sometimes they blend in, sometimes they intrude, occasionally they become lifelong friends. My introduction would build to a thesis sentence, something like:

> Although many of the people in my neighborhood will probably fade from my memory over time, like the minor details of a setting, there are a few landmark neighbors whom I'll never forget.

The structure to follow is quite simple—three paragraphs, one for each memorable neighbor. As always, my goal is to provide vivid and specific details that honor my reader—and my subjects—by creating a vivid portrait in words.

> One is Mr. Fryer, a ninety-six-year-old retired postman. Mr. Fryer suffers from terrible arthritis and has to walk in a horizontal position. I always know when he is coming by the sound of his oversize slippers shuffling along the path between his apartment and ours. He does his own marketing, though. Every afternoon at four o'clock, when I come home from school, Mr. Fryer sets out with his shopping cart, the successor to his mail cart, and lugs himself six blocks to the natural foods store on Beverly Boulevard. He moves about as fast as

an iceberg, and by the time he returns, there is just enough sunlight for him to slip his key into his front door. I once asked Mr. Fryer why he doesn't take a taxi to the market, and he said, "Taxis are for lazy people. When I'm ready for a ride somewhere, it'll be in a hearse."

Notice that the transitional topic sentence I chose—*One is Mr. Fryer, a ninety-six-year-old retired postman*—gets right to the point without being fancy. It may seem like an obvious transition to throw in, but it does place the reader in good hands, and a reader who feels safe stays along for the whole ride.

I'm about to use another straightforward transitional topic sentence as I introduce Mrs. Rubin: *Another neighbor I will never forget is Mrs. Rubin.* I didn't choose this obvious transition because I couldn't think of anything else; I chose it deliberately, to repeat a clause from my thesis sentence (*there are a few landmark neighbors whom I'll never forget*). This simple repetition is like the voice of the pilot breaking in during a flight. It reminds the passengers—in our case, the readers—that a human being is awake and flying the plane. "Ladies and gentlemen, this is your thesis statement speaking . . . just wanted to make myself heard again so that you know the next stretch of our flight is part of the plan."

Since I opened the paragraph with a simple sentence, I'll continue with a complex one: *Whenever I see Mrs. Rubin, I react in one of two ways: turn and run, or turn and run.* Alternating between long and short—or among simple, compound, and complex—is one way to please the reader's ear. Remember that writing is like composing music: sometimes your ear craves a long, gradual, and winding rhythm, and sometimes it craves a swift one. It's this interplay between rhythms that can make your writing sing.

My goal is also a little comedy, so I'll use *in the first case* and *in the second case* to emphasize that both cases produce the same result: me running away. Now I have to explain why:

In the first case, I turn and run because she is on foot, which means she is not on her way to a doctor's appointment and has plenty of time to talk. In the second case, I turn and run because she is behind the wheel of her car, a fact that puts my life in danger. Behind the wheel Mrs. Rubin is like a blind person testing the road ahead, only instead of a cane, she uses her bumper. Her driving technique could best be described as go-and-stop: first she goes, then she stops to listen for a crash. If all she hears is a cacophony of honking horns—and not the crunch of metal on metal—she barrels forward again, then stops to listen. Fortunately for Mrs. Rubin, she still drives the last new car she bought: a 1970 Plymouth Valiant, a heavy sedan with an extremely long hood.

I'm ready to introduce my third neighbor. To keep my structure holy, I'll give her her own paragraph. But this time I'll choose a gentler, rising transitional topic sentence: *No matter how far away I move, I'll never escape my third memorable neighbor, Joy.* The syllable pattern alone sets this sentence apart from the opening sentences of the first two paragraphs. Try tapping it out as you read. Notice how the beat gets a running start, leaps, and then thuds on the final word: *Joy*. I want to land hard on her name, in part for the sound, but also because I'm about to highlight the irony of such a name belonging to such a neighbor: *Joy is the most unpleasant lady I have ever known.*

As the paragraph moves into an anecdote about Joy's unpleasantness, notice the transition words of time that keep it moving:

> A smile on her face is as rare as a snowfall on Santa Monica beach, yet she did manage to make it snow, one Christmas Day, right on our front lawn. A new tenant in our building, unaware of Joy's request that we not wheel our trash cans on her side of the hedge, had received an enormous care package from his mother for the holidays. The UPS-delivered box was bulging with his favorite foods, each one lovingly wrapped and all of them cushioned by hundreds of white Styrofoam crescents. On trash day, when the new tenant dragged his box to the curb, he discovered it wouldn't fit on our side of the hedge, so he chose the wider path on Joy's side. At the bottom of the box, a small crack permitted several pieces of Styrofoam to dribble onto Joy's lawn. The next morning, we woke up to a white Christmas: six inches of Styrofoam crescents, the result of a Joyful rage, blanketed our front yard.

The transition words and phrases *one* (in *one Christmas Day*), *on trash day,* and *the next morning* escort the reader through the story about Joy's hedge rage. Keep in mind that I didn't look at a chart of transition words and then decide, "Gee, I think I'll use *yet* for a transition here." The transition words come out naturally, during writing, because the impulse to organize and classify things is as innate as the lust for junk food.

Do all transitions have to come in the form of a statement? Certainly not. Once in a while a rhetorical question can be your bridge from one idea to the next. Should you use them all the time? Certainly not.

Transition Words and Phrases

To compare:	also	besides	other
	and	in addition to	moreover
	another	similarly	too
	equally	like	just as
To contrast:	although	instead	otherwise
	but	nevertheless	still
	however	on the other hand	yet
	in spite of	as opposed to	unlike
	by contrast	though	whereas
To give an example:	for example	for instance	one
	exemplifies	shows	indication
	one example	another example	indicates
			suggests
To show cause and effect:	as a result	because	consequently
	for	since	so
	so that	therefore	thus

To indicate time:	after	finally	next
	at last	first	then
	at once	before	thereafter
	eventually	later	when
	soon	just then	suddenly
To specify where:	above	from	next
	across	here	on
	around	in	over
	before	inside	there
	behind	into	toward
	beyond	nearby	under
To show importance or classify:	first	primarily	then
	second	last	more
	to begin with	in addition	important
			furthermore
For variety:	pose a rhetorical question now and then		

Conclusion: The Party Favor You Give Your Guests

If you host a dinner party in your own home, what do you when a guest has to leave? Do you say, "Thanks for coming; you can let yourself out," or "Thanks for coming; I'll walk you to the door"? If you don't really like the guest and never plan on inviting him back, then the first choice is the correct approach. But if you hope he'll attend another of your dinner parties, or if you want to be polite, the second choice is better.

A good writer, like a good host, escorts the reader out, even gives him a party favor at the door. That gentle, affectionate good-bye is the conclusion to your multiparagraph essay. It should wrap things up, offer a parting idea, and leave the reader with a desire to return:

> I have a lot of anxiety about leaving this neighborhood. I live in mortal fear of Mrs. Rubin pulling out of her garage just as Mr. Fryer is puttering across Kings Road with his cart full of groceries, while Joy, seething over some imagined slight by the old man, decides not to warn him. The thought of his free-range eggs getting splattered on the sidewalk—or worse, of Mr. Fryer himself getting splattered there—has kept me rooted on North Kings Road for the last five years. Of course, I can't stand guard over the neighborhood forever: soon my daughter's toys will accumulate so high, I won't even be able to see out the window.
>
> And so I'd better start packing. I won't have to pack my neighbors, though: they're already tucked away someplace permanent, in these words.

You're Entitled to a Title

Do you remember your first pet? It could have been a stuffed animal, a goldfish you won at the fair, or an injured bird you brought home with the noble intention of saving a life. The stuffed animal might have been one of many lined up in a corner of your bed and eventually forgotten underneath it. But I'll bet you gave it a name. The goldfish certainly wasn't the most vociferous member of the family, but neither was it anonymous. And the injured bird was likely to be dead by morning, but when you buried it in the backyard, it had a tombstone, didn't it? And that tombstone had a name.

Human beings love to name things, especially the things we create. Artists name their paintings and sculptures. Songwriters name their songs, poets their poems, parents their kids. This naming instinct avoids confusion. (When my daughter says she wants to sleep with Alabaster, I know which stuffed bunny she means.) It also strengthens our attachment to the thing we've named by making it more vivid and, in a sense, more ours.

For the essay about my neighbors, I considered several titles. One was "Joyless Joy." I decided against that title because it emphasized Joy over the other neighbors, and I didn't want to give her center stage. Another title I thought of was "From My Window" because it fit the image in the conclusion of me watching over Mr. Fryer. But since most of the essay takes place outside my apartment—in the alley, on the sidewalk, along the hedge—I decided to look for a better title. The one I settled on isn't fancy, but it has a nice ring: "On North Kings Road."

When you write an essay, poem, story, or song, don't forget to honor it by giving it a name. It doesn't have to be a long name or even a terribly clever one. Sometimes a simple title is best. But a piece of writing without a title is like a dog without tags: easy to lose sight of, hard to get back once it's gone.

A House That Cannot Fall

Early on the morning of January 18, 1994, I was jolted out of bed by an earthquake. It was Martin Luther King Day, and I had planned on sleeping in—a rare treat for a teacher on a Monday morning. The earthquake was so severe and lasted so long, I was convinced that my apartment building on North Kings Road would crumble, and I would be crushed to death.

But when the quake finally exhausted itself, the building stood still—and still stood. Through the narrow field of my flashlight's vision, I surveyed the damage. In the hallway the doorbell chimes were still clattering like nervous bones. In the living room books had shot out of their shelves like spit teeth; a side table had been flipped onto its back, legs up, in surrender; and the television lay facedown in a puddle of its own glass. I aimed my light at the bay window: all sixty-four diamond-shaped panes were still intact. I pointed it at the fireplace: perfect posture. There wasn't a chunk of plaster or a paint chip on the floor.

The chimes settled down, and as silence fell over the apartment, I realized that the only damage this 6.7 earthquake had wrought was to my things—the furniture, decorations, and appliances I had brought with me when I moved in. The building itself, nearly sixty-five years old, hadn't flinched.

My friends who lived in newer apartments told a different story. They reported broken windows, gaping walls, tilting floors. One unhappy tenant told me she had had to lower herself out the window in order to leave her 1980s town house: the stairs had been knocked three feet from the front door.

But my stairs were made of stone. My front door was made of intricately etched unbreakable glass. And my front porch, also of stone, was edged by a pair of black wrought-iron rails, as solid as they were decorative.

What was the difference between my 1930s apartment building and the newer ones just blocks away? Mine had structure. It was built by true craftsmen using quality materials. It was built with careful planning and much pride. It was built to last.

Be a true craftsman when you write. Build your sentences, paragraphs, compositions, chapters, and books; your scenes, acts, and screenplays; your letters, love notes, and e-mails; your journal entries, graduation speeches, job applications, wedding vows, memoirs, and epitaphs—build all of these with solid structure. If you use quality language, careful planning, and much pride when you write, yours will be a house of words we can visit forever.

Six

Thou Shalt Describe Thy World, Express Thy Opinions, and Preserve Thy Past

SOMETIME IN THE MIDDLE OF EVERY OCTOBER in my childhood, my Auntie Hankie and Uncle Irving would come home from Europe. Their return was one of the rituals of our family life, and we marked it with their favorite American food: hamburgers.

While their plane was soaring high above the Rocky Mountains, my mother and I would be at Farmers Market, Third and Fairfax, buying food. First stop: the produce stall near Gate Two, for iceberg lettuce so crisp you could already hear it crunching in your mouth, and beefsteak tomatoes, plump and juicy and deep red. Then on to Thee's Continental Bakery for seven proud and buttery buns, big as a salad plate, that you had to slice yourself at home, the old-fashioned way. The last stop, so its results would remain fresh, was Marconda's Meats, where the leanest, most luscious ground round was displayed on silver trays at my eye level. I would watch the butcher's metal spatula plunge into the meat and scoop up, on his very first try, the exact quantity we needed: three and a half pounds. (The buns were so big that my father insisted on filling them with half-pounders for all.)

Although there were many tempting desserts for sale at Farmers Market, we walked right past them. In our kitchen at that very moment, while my aunt and uncle were beginning their descent, my father would be spreading chocolate icing on his Never-Fail Cake, a recipe that his mother had whispered to him before he left for the navy and that had made him many friends at sea.

The highlight of my aunt and uncle's annual return from Europe wasn't the presents they brought my brothers and me (although I did treasure the Marks & Spencer sweaters and Fortnum & Mason mints); it wasn't the hamburger feed or the Never-Fail Cake. (I was already leaning toward becoming a vegetarian, and I had licked the frosting from the bowl.) No, the highlight of their return was my aunt herself, a dazzling storyteller whose powers of description sent me on a first-class tour of the very cities from which she had just returned.

"It was cold in London," she would tell us. "On the first morning we looked out our hotel window and saw Hyde Park all covered with frost, as if it had grown white fur overnight. And at the antique market in Covent Garden, there was a man roasting chestnuts over a crackling tin can. We bought some just to warm our hands. Even the statue of Lord Nelson, towering over Trafalgar Square, looked as if he needed an overcoat."

This sort of vivid descriptive language poured out of my aunt's mouth and right into mine, which was wide with astonishment and delight and wanderlust. I swallowed her descriptions, saw them again that night in my dreams, and set out to see them with my own eyes when I turned seventeen and got the first stamp on my passport.

Ever since then, descriptive writing has been one of the first kinds of writing I teach my students to do.

Good Descriptive Writing: The Essentials

Have you seen the movie *Harold and Maude*? It's about a seventeen-year-old boy who falls in love with an eighty-year-old woman. She's coming to the end of her life, and he hasn't even begun to live his. She teaches him how. There is a wonderful scene in which Maude straps a breathing mask over Harold and turns on her odorifics device. She pops in a canister, pumps up the machine, and in a few moments Harold is treated to a smorgasbord of smells—from cigarettes to snow. Later she takes him to a field of sunflowers, teaches him to play the banjo, bakes him an oat straw pie, and lets him caress a wooden sculpture in her trailer. At one point Harold tells Maude he hasn't lived at all until he met her. She's awakened him, inspired him, and one way she's done it is by giving him a feast of the five senses.

You don't need an odorifics machine to seduce your reader; you can do it with words:

His voice had the soft throaty sound of a croaking frog and he seemed to speak all his words with an immense wet-lipped relish, as though they tasted good on the tongue.

—ROALD DAHL, pricking up our ears in "The Ratcatcher" [and reminding us that words taste good on the tongue].

The mud lay thick upon the stones, and a black mist hung over the streets; the rain fell sluggishly down, and everything felt cold and clammy to the touch.

—CHARLES DICKENS, giving us the feel of a wet London day in *Oliver Twist*. [Notice how the rain falls "sluggishly" down, an adverb that reflects the feeling we might have on such a dreary day.]

Fishiest of all fish places was the Try Pots, which well deserved its name; for the pots there were always boiling chowders. Chowder for breakfast, and chowder for dinner, and chowder for supper, till you began to look for fish-bones coming through your clothes. The area before the house was paved with clam-shells. Mrs. Hussey wore a polished necklace of codfish vertebra; and Hosea Hussey had his account books bound in superior old shark-skin. There was a fishy flavor to the milk, too, that I could not at all account for, till one morning happening to take a stroll along the beach among some fishermen's boats, I saw Hosea's brindled cow

feeding on fish remnants, and marching along the sand with
each foot in a cod's decapitated head.

   —HERMAN MELVILLE, *ruining our appetite*
in Moby-Dick. *[Notice how he keeps the fish theme*
running through the whole paragraph by having fishy
things everywhere, from the woman's necklace to the milk to
the hooves of the cow, where cod heads are worn like shoes.]

Language that appeals to the senses is called sensory language. It's one of the hallmarks of good descriptive writing
because it intensifies the experience of reading. Let's say you're
describing an odd smell you might encounter upon sniffing
a piece of rotten salmon. You could run to the thesaurus and
write, *It had the scent of putrefaction—septic, fusty, swampy—but I ate*
it anyway. This is an accurate description, but it uses a series of
adjectives to communicate what could be conveyed more mem-
orably by arousing the reader's nose: *It smelled like Play-Doh mari-*
nated in dead flower water, but I ate it anyway. Chances are most of
your readers don't know what *fusty* means, but who among us
hasn't had Play-Doh on our hands or emptied a vase of forgotten flowers?

If you want to add sensory language to your writing, start
collecting sensual words. Use your thesaurus to expand your
vocabulary of shape words (parabolic, oblong, boxy, oval,
vaulted, crescent, squat), size words (petit, scrawny, diminutive;
lofty, formidable, whopping), color words (chartreuse, amber,
cobalt, sable, grizzled, tawny, indigo, sienna), smell words (gamy,
pungent, acrid, foul, rancid, rank, putrid; fragrant, ambrosial,

floral, aromatic), sound words (plink, rumble, trill, creak, rattle, thump, whoosh, bang), taste words (sweet, sugary, candied, savory; sour, acidic, tangy, tart), and texture words (smooth, creamy, velvety, corrugated, spiky, fleecy, knobbed, gnarled, coarse). But remember to use the thesaurus for variety, not vanity. A parade of overdressed words will nauseate the reader, just as too much whipped cream can ruin a fresh berry pie.

Another essential of descriptive writing is figurative language. Figurative language is like an inside joke that everybody gets. It strengthens the bond between writer and reader by comparing the thing you describe to something else that your reader already knows.

Since all readers are human, one effective kind of figurative language is personification, or giving human qualities to things. As an exercise in descriptive writing, I take my students around the school and tell them to make friends with a tree. Their goal is to describe the tree as if it were a human being—to personify it. One student chose the oak tree that stands at the edge of our basketball court. He described it as *the team's secret weapon, a center with long arms reaching out to block even the best player's shots.* Another student selected a silver maple at the back of the yard. She described it as "leaning against the fence, just waiting for someone to come along and chat."

When my daughter and I go to the Beverly Hills Public Library, we often drive along Burton Way, a wide street with a promenade separating the east- and west-bound traffic. At the end of the promenade stands a group of very tall, very thin palm trees. We call them the Lean Family—not just because they are so thin, but because they seem to be craning to one side or the other, trying to get the best view of downtown. By personifying this family of trees, we give them a permanent place in our memories, in our minds.

Langston Hughes wrote:

Hold fast to dreams
For if dreams die
Life is a broken-winged bird
That cannot fly.

Hold fast to dreams
For when dreams go
Life is a barren field
Frozen with snow.

I love this poem for two reasons: the metaphor in the first stanza and the metaphor in the second. A metaphor is a type of figurative language that shows how two things are alike by saying that one *is* the other. We know that a life without dreams isn't really a broken-winged bird, but they do have something in common: both are desperate. Now, Langston Hughes could have written, "Hold fast to your dreams / For if dreams die / Life is desperate." But that wouldn't be nearly as pleasurable for the reader. What makes it pleasurable is that the reader can actually *feel* the desperation by *picturing* the broken-winged bird and the barren, snowbound field.

The English poet W. H. Auden had the sort of face you see once and never forget. Deep creases ran across his forehead, under his sagging eyes, and down his plump cheeks. When asked to describe this rugged, timeworn face of his, the poet replied, "It is like a wedding cake left out in the rain."

Auden's description uses another type of figurative language, the simile. Like a metaphor, a simile compares two very different things that have one important feature in common. Unlike a metaphor, though, a simile uses *as* or *like* to suggest the connection.

Now you might wonder what a rain-soaked wedding cake has to do with a man's face. A face isn't food. A cake can't smile or frown. But this particular face did have something in common with a sodden wedding cake: both were once firm and symmetrical and pristine. Age had tugged at Auden's taut features, made them slip and sag, just as the optimistic swirls on a fresh wedding cake would sink and stretch and deflate in the rain. It's a far-fetched comparison, but when crafting a good simile, the farther-fetched the more surprising, and the more surprising the more delightful. You want your simile to be as unforgettable as the thing it describes.

A student of mine once described her classmate's ears as being *shaped like auditoriums, with crumbs of wax on the stage.* It was a striking simile, first of all because it's true (look at your own ear in the mirror: the hole is the stage and the ridges are the rows of seats); second of all, because everyone can relate to it (we've all got ears, and we've all sat in auditoriums); and third of all, because none of us had ever noticed it before (we'd been too busy scratching our ears to examine them).

When you write a simile or metaphor, be sure you do the figurative language check. First ask yourself if it's universal. If you've written the sentence, *My neighbor has a terrible voice; she sings like my brother,* you're in trouble. Unless the reader is a member of your family or a close friend, he can't possibly know how your brother sings. But if you've written, *My neighbor has a terrible voice; she sings like a turkey the week before Thanksgiving,* this is a gobble we've all either heard or can imagine.

The second simile check is to make sure it is true. If you are describing your pet horned toad, for example, it might be a good idea to avoid the simile *his back was as rough as polished marble.* Your reader will react in one of two ways: (1) this guy's a moron; he doesn't know that polished marble is smooth; or (2) this guy's an animal abuser; he's been using sandpaper on the back of his toad. The first reaction will get your essay thrown in the trash; the second will get you thrown in jail.

Avoid crowding your similes too. A well-crafted simile has something important to say, just as each of my students has something important to say. But when my students all speak at once, the only sound they make is noise. Since your similes can't raise their hands, you have to safeguard their uniqueness for them by following this general rule: rarely more than two in a sentence, three in a paragraph, five per page.

And if you don't want your reader to roll her eyes in disgust, keep the clichés out of your pen. A cliché is the language equivalent of an aging uncle in the family who tells the same stories over and over again. "Stop me if you've heard this," he begins, and you *have,* about a hundred times, but you can't stop him because he's your uncle, and even if you were to say you've heard it before, he'd find someone else in the room who hasn't.

Clichés are *as universal as taxes, as true as love;* they were once *as bright as the sun,* but they have been said so many times that they've gotten *as old as rotten eggs*. If you write clichés, the reaction you will get will be *as cold as ice*. Your reader might *roar like a lion* or *scream like a banshee,* unless of course he is as *sweet as sugar, as cute as pie,* or *as dumb as a doorknob*.

The difference between your uncle and a cliché is that you *can* stop a cliché from speaking. Of course, you have a major disadvantage in your battle against clichés: you might not recognize them. You probably haven't lived as long as, say, your storytelling uncle, so how can you be expected to know a cliché if you write one? The best way to develop an ear for clichés (as well as for originality) is to read as much as you can. There is also that most useful weapon in any battle, the one you are developing every day—experience.

Three Types of Descriptive Writing

1. Description of a Thing

It had been wrought, as was easy to perceive, with wonderful skill of needlework; and the stitch (as I am assured by ladies conversant with such mysteries) gives evidence of a now forgotten art, not to be recovered even by the process of picking out the threads. This rag of scarlet cloth,—for time, and wear, and a sacrilegious moth, had reduced it to little other than a rag,—on careful examination, assumed the shape of a letter. It was the capital letter A.

—NATHANIEL HAWTHORNE,
The Scarlet Letter

A street musician carries his guitar around with him like an extra limb. A lady sits on the grass at an outdoor concert, the parrot on her shoulder bobbing to the beat. An old man shuffles home from the market, pushing a rusty basket on wheels. A teenager glides through a mall on her Razor scooter. A grandfather sits on a porch swing, filling his pipe with tobacco and tamping it down with his thumb. A toddler panics when something falls from her lap; her mother scoops up a shiny silk blankie and hands it back: the toddler is calm.

What do you remember about each of these brief scenes? Is it the musician or his guitar, the lady or her parrot, the old man or his rolling basket? Maybe you have a grandfather, and every time you picture him, he's smoking his pipe or leaning on his cane. Maybe you have a little brother or sister who won't go anywhere without a security blanket. Maybe you yourself won't go anywhere without your scooter. The objects we delight in or depend on can be so much a part of who we are that they become our identifying features, or attributes, as sure as a birthmark or the tilt of our nose.

When I assign a description of a thing, I ask my students to describe an object that has a strong association for them, the one thing they hope to inherit from their parents, the one thing they would save from a fire or reach back in time and pull from the trash. As with all descriptive writing, the goal is to put the object in the reader's hand by using rich sensory language. It is also to provide a context that will show why the object matters so much.

The object I chose is my mother's purse.

TOPIC: DESCRIBE ONE OBJECT THAT YOU'LL
NEVER FORGET FROM YOUR CHILDHOOD.
PROVIDE A CONTEXT, OR STORY, TO GO WITH IT.

Purse Strings and Ice Creams

To this day, I can't smell a stick of Juicy Fruit gum without feeling like I've committed a crime. The gum was
what helped my mother stay away from her addiction:
cigarettes. And the place where she kept the gum was
her red vinyl purse, an object from my childhood that
I'll never forget. She kept her money there too, which
made it my destination every afternoon at four o'clock.
To get there I had to move slowly across her bedroom
floor to her desk, but not so slowly that I'd miss the Ice
Cream Man, whose truck would be arriving at any
minute with *my* addiction.

I could always find my mother's purse, not by the
scent of leather—this was the early 1970s, when her
politics prevented her from buying dead animal products—but by the reflection of afternoon sunlight on its
plastic-coated red vinyl. It had a tiny gold latch made of
two interlocking balls. Slyly I would twist them apart,
open the purse, and smell a pungent bouquet of lipstick, Juicy Fruit, and the Estée Lauder Youth Dew perfume that always preceded my mother when she entered
a room and lingered after she'd gone.

With one ear listening for the toilet to flush (I bur-
gled while she piddled) and the other listening for the
Ice Cream Man, I would reach past packs of gum, pos-

sibly used Kleenex, and six different pairs of glasses, one for each of my mother's changing moods, indoors and out. As the tinkling would ease to a trickle, I would reach the pot of gold at the bottom of the bag: her change purse. Another latch twisted open, and I'd start plucking coins one at a time, removing them silently, like body parts in the game of Operation.

A flush from the bathroom, the jaunty, kid-friendly tune from my favorite truck, and the pounding of my own guilty heart would be the soundtrack to the next twenty seconds. I would pocket the change, wipe the makeup from my fingers, and latch the purse shut. Then I would pray for my mother to turn the faucet on, and when she did, the water splashing onto her hands would muffle my footsteps out of the room.

Once in a while, her voice would call out, "Honey, would you buy me a root beer Popsicle?" And in exchange for her silence about my crime, I would.

OUTLINE FOR DESCRIPTION OF A THING
(GOAL: USE SENSORY LANGUAGE AND
CONTEXT TO SHOW IMPORTANCE.)

I.   Introduction: topic sentence mentions the object (mother's purse)
     Context established (stole from it to buy ice cream)

II. Description
     A. Begin with most eye-catching feature (shiny red vinyl)

B. How it felt to the touch (interlocking gold balls)

C. Scent (Juicy Fruit, cigarettes, makeup, and Youth Dew perfume)

D. Context continued through sounds (mother in bathroom, ice cream truck)

E. More tactile features as the hand goes in (gum, Kleenex, glasses)

F. More description of objects within (change purse, coins)

III. Context developed (toilet flushes; tension of thief trying to escape)

IV. Conclusion and twist (Mom knows he's stealing, asks for a Popsicle)

For your description of an important object, you might settle on a stuffed animal, a favorite shirt, or a good luck charm you latched on to as a kid. You might have won an award or a trophy that has special significance for you. You might remember something absurd, like the signature-filled cast you kept from the time you broke an arm. Or you might remember something poignant, like the tags worn by your now-departed dog.

2. *Description of a Place*

And now to the cemetery—graveyard—burying ground—that is the site of most, but not all, of the skulduggeries that follow. It lies behind Oysterville, on a ridge. The immediately surrounding area is in parts impassable by reason of a mad growth of plants ranging from spruce, hemlock and fir to ferns, salal, gorse, Scotch broom and evergreen blackberry bushes. Crows caw interminably; gulls scream and wheel; smaller birds, hidden among bushes and branches, repeat personal remarks. The trees murmur among themselves. When the rain falls hard, or the wind turns mean, they sigh and hunch, as cattle or horses might in an exposed field. In quick showers, there is a sound from the undergrowth like tiny feet running.

—WILLARD ESPY,
Skulduggery on Shoalwater Bay

But the house on Mango Street is not the way they told it at all. It's small and red with tight steps in front and windows so small you'd think they were holding their breath.

—SANDRA CISNEROS,
The House on Mango Street

At some point in your school career, you will be asked to write a description of a place. It may be a place you vacationed, a place you got lost, or a place where you had to overcome a challenge. If you're lucky, you'll be asked to describe a funny place like the trunk of your dad's car, the inside of a locker, or your sister's bedroom after she's been grounded for a week. Some teachers want you to describe your school, your neighborhood, or your home. They're not being nosy; they're just offering you a familiar setting on which to practice your powers of description.

Practice them well. Good descriptive writing is a treat for the senses. Try to indulge all five. Season your descriptions with similes and metaphors, but remember to do the figurative language check for universality, truth, and originality.

One helpful tip for describing a place is to write from an unusual point of view. "Point of view" refers to who or what is speaking. In *Skulduggery on Shoalwater Bay* Willard Espy writes a series of poems from the point of view of the dead, a truly underground collection. *Black Beauty* is told from the point of view of a horse, *The Call of the Wild* from that of a dog. If asked to describe your neighborhood, for example, you might choose to do it from the point of view of an owl, the mailman, or the tallest tree on your street. You might describe a contemporary mall from Don Quixote's point of view, or an operating room through the eyes of Leonardo da Vinci. Remember that readers like variety, and one way to provide it is to offer them an unexpected point of view.

TOPIC: DESCRIBE A ROOM IN YOUR HOUSE
FROM AN UNUSUAL POINT OF VIEW.
FIND A CONTEXT TO MAKE THE
DESCRIPTION MEANINGFUL

A Messy Kitchen—All for Me

I used to be an only child. They took me with them everywhere they went. I got to sleep in their bed and eat scrambled eggs for breakfast. I got to curl up with them on the couch when they watched TV. And I got to stand at the window and shout at everyone who walked by.

That firstborn treatment dried up the day *she* came

home. I was two at the time, and they shipped me off to the grandparents for a week. When I was permitted to return, they greeted me with a warm and loving "STOP THAT BARKING! YOU'LL WAKE THE BABY!"

Her name is Sophie, and she turned four on June 6 this year, nearly a month before *my* birthday, which hasn't been celebrated around here since she arrived. But last week, on the first of July, when Dad and I returned from our morning run, I saw an amazing sight: the kitchen was a mess.

The black-and-white checkerboard floor was dusted with flour, as though a blast of snow had come in through an open window. The sink was a jumble of stacked bowls, measuring cups, and a wire whisk. On the countertop flecks of grated cheese sat between the tiles, tantalizingly out of reach. The trash can was in plain view, and when I rose on my hind legs to have a sniff, I saw cracked egg shells, empty wrappers of sliced cheese, and a chicken bone. On top of the stove stood their old-fashioned windup timer, ticking like a heartbeat. They're at it again, I thought, cooking up something really savory for themselves but off limits to me.

Ding went the timer, and out it came: the rich aroma of warmed chicken, melted cheddar, and cooked eggs. They'd messed up *my* kitchen to make themselves a souf-flé! And when they'd sit down to eat it, if I asked for a taste, they'd say, "No begging, Lucy. Finish your kibble."

But as the soufflé cooled, I smelled an appetizing blend of barley, lamb, and brown sugar. What was one of my dog biscuits doing in there? Then I saw Sophie, the four-year-old twerp, reach for my bag of jerky treats. She slid the jerky treat into the top of the soufflé like a birthday candle. She reached for another, and another, and then two more. She even remembered the one for good luck. By the time she was through, a total of six treats rose up from that soufflé like soldiers saluting their general—and the general was me!

"Happy birthday to you," they sang. "Happy birthday to you! Happy birthday, dear Lucy, happy birthday to you!"

I couldn't help it—my tail began to wag. I looked over at Dad still in his running shorts. His face was half-hidden behind the video camera, the same video camera he had pointed at Sophie less than a month before, when she was blowing out the candles on *her* cake.

"Happy birthday, Lucy," Dad said from behind the camera.

"It was Sophie's idea to bake you a cake," Mom said.

Sophie's idea? The little twerp who had stolen my place in their bed, who had ten times the number of toys that I had, who got to pee inside and play with the hose outside? *That* little twerp? God bless her, she did what I thought no one would ever be able to do again—she brought me back into the family.

I didn't blow out the candles. I bit the tops off instead. Then I took one last look at the kitchen. What a glorious mess! And all for me.

OUTLINE FOR DESCRIPTION OF A PLACE
(GOALS: WRITE FROM AN UNUSUAL POINT OF VIEW;
USE SENSORY LANGUAGE.)
(NOTE: THE SPECIFIC CHOICES I MADE ARE IN
PARENTHESES; YOU CAN USE THE SAME STRUCTURE
AND PLUG IN YOUR OWN SPECIFICS.)

I.   Introduction. Establish the point of view (the dog), the tone (grumpy because demoted by the kid), and the context (birthdays). Notice that it's okay to write the introduction in several short paragraphs instead of a single long one. Arrive at the location in the thesis sentence (*the kitchen was a mess*).

II.   Pick one of the reader's five senses and entertain it (the sense of sight). Use transition words of space to organize the description (*to the left of . . . on top of . . . on the floor,* etc.) Use figurative language when possible (*as though a blast of snow had come through an open window*).

III. Entertain another sense (sound—the ticking and the DING of the timer).

IV.   Another sense (smell—as the oven door opens). Notice that you don't have to write for all five senses every time. (This essay leaves out the sense of taste, but by the end the reader knows the dog will enjoy her birthday feast.)

V.   Transition toward conclusion (the soufflé is turning into a birthday cake).

VI.   Conclusion. Bring back an idea from the introduction
       (the dog's resentment toward the kid turns to affection).
       Give the reader a sense that the essay is finished (the dog
       bites off the candle tips) and that it's okay to leave (dog is
       happy now).

The joy of writing from a point of view other than your
own is like the joy of being an actor: you get to "play" many different parts, and each one widens your perspective and invites
you to alter your voice. The basic facts of the description above
are true. Sophie did urge us to make a birthday cake for our dog
Lucy; my wife actually baked the strange concoction I described;
and the kitchen really was a mess. (I had to clean it up.) But by
writing the description from Lucy's point of view, I forced
myself to see the world as she sees it: curmudgeonly, a little left
out, but finally grateful to have a human sibling with a big imagination and an equally big heart.

3. Description of a Face

*His yellow skin scarcely covered the work of muscles and arteries
beneath; his hair was of a lustrous black, and flowing; his teeth of
a pearly whiteness; but these luxuriances only formed a more hor-
rid contrast with his watery eyes, that seemed almost of the same
colour as the dun white sockets in which they were set, his shriv-
elled complexion and straight black lips.*

—MARY SHELLEY,
Frankenstein

"Reach in the bag and take a face, but don't look at it 'til you sit down." It is face-painting day in English class, and this is how I greet students as they file in. The faces they choose are not their own, and the materials they'll use are not brushes and paint. The faces come from the glossy pages of magazines; the paint will come from their pens.

When they all have a face in hand, I tell them to study it. "Take notes on what you see. Try to compare the facial features to things outside the face (food, nature, household items, animals). Make your similes and metaphors as outrageous as possible. But make them true. Any questions?"

"I don't like the face I got. Can I trade it in for another?"

"Nope, you're stuck with it. Just like you're stuck with the one you saw in the mirror this morning."

Once the class settles in, my favorite sound in the world fills the room: the living, breathing silence of twenty minds at work. Beneath the silence the tread of pen or pencil on paper begins. I walk up and down the rows, glancing at the photographs and the words beginning to describe them. *Teeth like a falling-down picket fence. Hair like a frozen wave. Eyes like chocolate drops floating in a glass of milk.*

One pencil is moving faster than all the rest. But it's not writing. It's twirling rapidly, a spinner in search of an idea. The student is stuck.

"I can't think of anything," she says.

I look at the face in the picture. It is of an old, old man, with cotton white hair and deeply etched lines across his forehead and down his face. He looks a little like Robert Frost.

"He's got an interesting forehead," I say. "What do you notice about it?"

"It's old."

"How do you know?"

"It's got lines, I guess."

"They remind you of anything?"

"My grandfather has the same ones."

"We've never seen your grandfather. Do you they remind you of anything we have seen?"

"Clouds."

"What kind?"

"The squiggly ones you see from far away."

"Write that down," I tell her. "They're called cirrus clouds if you want to use the word. But you don't have to. *The squiggly clouds you see from far away* is a good description.

"His eyes look kind of like frosted glass."

"That's another good one. Keep going."

And she does. Twenty minutes later her hand comes up. "Can I read mine first?" she asks. "As soon as you revise it," I answer. When most of the students have finished, I invite them to trade with a neighbor, proofread each other's work, and polish their own.

After the students have read their magazine descriptions out loud, and just before the bell rings, I tell them to take a good look around the room. "Tomorrow you're going to describe one of your classmates." You can hardly hear the bell above their nervous groan.

OUTLINE FOR DESCRIPTION OF A FACE
(GOALS: USE BOLD SIMILES AND METAPHORS;
MAKES A LOGICAL SWEEP DOWN THE FACE;
PUT A TWIST IN THE CONCLUSION.)

I.   Introduction. Mention the name of your subject. Try to plant a little detail you will return to in the conclusion. Follow the topic sentence by going right into the description. Be logical in the order you choose. It makes sense to start with the shape of the head and work your way on to the face.

II.   Shape of head/face. Use a shape word (oblong, round, boxy, square, oval) and/or compare the shape to something else. Continue with prominent features—forehead, eyes, eyebrows, eyelashes, glasses (if worn), ears, nose, mouth, lips, teeth, cheeks, and chin.

III. More features. You can do all the features in paragraph II, or you can break them into two paragraphs. It depends on how much you have to write, and which features you want to focus on.

IV.   The most outstanding feature. It's a good idea to identify one unforgettable part of the person's face and give it its own paragraph.

V.   Conclusion. Call back to something from the intro.

The next day each student is assigned another student to write about. The only rule I impose about describing a live face is that they can't offend anyone. I enforce this rule by giving the subject veto power. A student once asked if she could describe the pockmark at the top of my forehead as a footprint left by a miniature deer. I thought that was a delightful image and said sure. But when she wanted to describe my goatee as a little accident that the deer had while prancing across my face, I told her to think of something else.

Here is a description of a girl written by a boy. Notice the elaborate similes he uses to describe her face. Notice also the structure he follows, beginning at the top of her head and ending at the birthmark on her neck.

TOPIC: DESCRIBE THE FACE OF ONE OF YOUR CLASSMATES. SEASON YOUR DESCRIPTION WITH FIGURES OF SPEECH.

Now I Know
by
Todd Wilson

Janelle is a pretty girl in my class who I think is eleven years old. She has long blond hair that reminds me of spaghetti with a touch of butter sauce. She keeps it very nice and brushed and usually wears a headband, but her bangs sometimes spill over.

Her face is narrow and the size of a pineapple without the spiky stuff on it. For eyes she has big brown chocolate kisses with almonds in the middle. Her eyes are joyful, and when you are talking to her, they look straight at you like she's paying total attention. Her eyebrows are thick and brown like matching commas that tripped and fell on their sides. Her eyelashes are long and brown. She wears glasses as big as half-dollars with mustard on the edge.

Janelle's nose is straight as a capital *A*. Her lips are medium-size and look like small pillows covered with red wax. Her oval ears are usually hidden behind her hair, but when they do show, they are fragile-looking.

Janelle has a very interesting birthmark on her neck, but there is a touch of it on her left cheek too. It sort of looks like the birth mark fell from the sky, bounced off her cheek, and left a little smudge there before landing on her neck.

I always thought Janelle was a pretty girl. But now that I've described her face, I know why.

I have to tell you that Todd was not an A student in English. His backpack looked like the sock drawer of a bachelor or the backseat of a minivan on the way home from a camping trip. Disorganized and a dreamer, Todd had a hard time remembering when the next quiz was, let alone what he should study for it. He was a lethargic note-taker who spent more time sharpening his pencil than actually using it. And at three-fifteen, while the other kids were zipping up their backpacks, Todd would be slowly unzipping his and then filling it with the wrong books for the next day.

I am glad that Todd dawdled at the end of class. It gave me a chance to tell him, in private, what a wonderful writer I thought he was.

Persuasive Writing

The art of persuasion is the ability to sway someone's opinion, not by taking a swing at his head but by taking logic to his mind. When my students get into a debate, they raise their hands, not their voices. They make their points calmly, support them logically, consider the other side and try to shoot it down, and then conclude. If everyone adheres to the rules of debate, we're able to have lively discussions about school uniforms, capital and corporal punishment, medical testing on animals, private versus public education—just about any topic that gets us fired up—but we never let ourselves burn out of control.

Of all the forms of writing you can learn, persuasive writing gives you the most power. Use it to request a longer recess, a later bedtime, or a shorter school year. Use it to get a skateboard park built in your neighborhood or a basketball court in your backyard. It's your best weapon against an unfair rule, an overbearing teacher, or an inedible burrito in the school cafeteria.

Can you imagine getting so fed up with your parents that you decided to leave home? Would you send them a letter explaining why you're out of there? Thomas Jefferson did. When he and the Founding Fathers had had enough of British rule, they chose to form their own government, and they sent a note to King George explaining why. That note was the Declaration of Independence, a model of persuasive writing:

When, in the course of human events, it becomes necessary for one people to dissolve the political bands which have connected them with another, and to assume, among the powers of the earth, the separate and equal station to which the laws of nature and of nature's God entitle them, a decent respect to the opinions of mankind requires that they should declare the causes which impel them to the separation.

There's not a trace of rancor or resentment in the tone. But this opening statement is filled with confidence. What follows is a logical and persuasive explanation of why the Founding Fathers felt it was time to form a republic of their own. Now, just because persuasive writing is based in logic doesn't mean it can't incite a war. King George's response to Jefferson's good-bye was to send over British troops. But he sent them, in part, because he feared the power of Jefferson's pen.

When I teach persuasive writing, I give my students a choice of topics. Since I want them to write with controlled passion, I like them to start with the passion and use structure to provide the control. Here is a sample persuasive essay on a subject many students can relate to:

TOPIC: SHOULD STUDENTS WEAR UNIFORMS AT SCHOOL?

Creativity, not Uniformity

Students should not have to wear uniforms at school. First of all, the uniforms are uncomfortable. They are made of high-content polyester or low-grade wool, fabrics to get stressed in, not dressed in. A student in uniform cannot play sports comfortably during recess and lunchtime. The girls are forced to wear skirts and knee-high socks, a combination that makes them feel self-conscious on the basketball court or soccer field. The boys, too, are constricted from moving freely in their tight-fitting wool pants, polyester shirts, and mandatory ties. Students who exert themselves in such uncomfortable clothes take longer to settle down when they return to class. Thus, the uniforms are not only uncomfortable; they interfere with learning.

Another point against school uniforms is their expense. A typical boy's uniform of two pairs of slacks, three white shirts, a blazer, and a pair of ties can cost a family nearly $500. Add to that the cost of the required black shoes and dry cleaning of the blazer, and the annual expense grows to over $750—all for a wardrobe that can't be worn during afternoons and weekends. Moreover, during the rapid-growth years of adolescence, a uniform bought in September often won't fit by March, and some families will have to buy a new set of clothes.

Most important, school uniforms limit creative expression. Our bodies aren't the only thing in a growth spurt; our minds are too. As Alison Lurie remarks in *The Language of Clothes,* "To choose clothes, either in a store or at home, is to define and describe ourselves" (p. 5). Yet uniforms do the defining and describing for us. They turn us into the equivalent of tract houses, one student indistinguishable from the next, and all of us deprived of the inalienable right to free speech through free dress.

Some people claim that uniforms camouflage our socioeconomic backgrounds. By requiring all students to dress alike, a school sets a standard of nondiscrimination based on social class. But while we may not wear our wealth on our sleeves, it is written all over the cars that we get in and out of each day. Besides, if students had free dress, those without money could make a positive impression with their sense of style, shopping at thrift stores or even making clothes of their own. The rule of uniforms deprives those students of an important outlet for their creativity—and inlet for new friends.

The idea of requiring uniforms may have been well intentioned, but in practice its intention is lost. Uniforms add stress to students and their families; they limit concentration; and they eliminate creativity. In conclusion, we come to school to have our minds expanded, not straitjacketed in prisons of wool.

Instead of an outline here, the drawing on the next page will guide you through a persuasive essay.

You start out as the little guy at the bottom of the stairs. Your goal is to come up with three distinct points, support each one with examples and explanations, consider the other side and shoot it down, and finally write a snappy conclusion. If you can accomplish all that in a single essay, you turn into the happy guy who's climbed the stairs, and you deserve a rest.

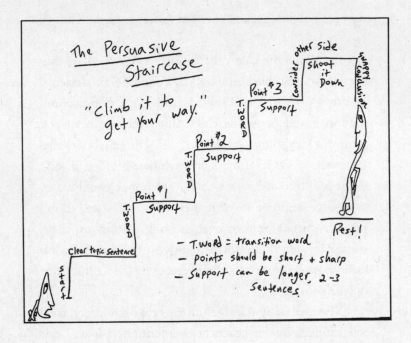

George Schoenman taught us that no argument is convincing that uses biased language—language that demeans the other side. In an argument against school uniforms, for example, you shouldn't write, *Anyone who thinks school uniforms are a good idea is a fashion moron who doesn't know a polka dot from a pleat.* This is name-calling at its most flagrant; it weakens your argument by undermining your authority as a writer. The more rational you sound, the more convincing you will be.

Narrative Writing

Persuasive writing is to your opinions what narrative writing is to your past. By telling stories, you entertain your listener; by writing them down, you preserve yourself. Imagine how much of your past would never be forgotten if you wrote about the following topics: *How My Parents Met; My Earliest Memory; My First Kiss; An Accident That Happened; My Most Embarrassing Moment; The Worst Thing I Ever Did; The Most Frightened I've Ever Been; The Bravest I've Ever Had to Be.*

My daughter goes to preschool in Beverly Glen Canyon, a twenty-minute ride from our apartment on North Kings Road. The daily commute could be tedious, but for me it's a treat: the moment I put the car into drive, I hear a plea from the backseat: "Daddy, tell me a story about when you were little." I've told her about the time I rode my bike down Laurel Canyon without my parents' permission. I've told her about the time Mannix, our childhood dog, got stuck in our chain-link fence. She's heard about the house across the street catching fire twice in one night. She's heard how her grandpa chased down a pair of neighbors who had the audacity to steal a tree from our front yard. (The tree was growing in a pot; the neighbors were drunk.)

I haven't told her about the time I rode my bicycle off a cliff, or the time I nearly electrocuted myself by cutting the cord of an electric blanket, or the time I almost died from spinal meningitis when I was six months old. These stories fall into the category of possibly traumatizing tales that I am saving until she is full grown.

During our car rides to preschool, Sophie has taught me a

lot about narrative writing. Through the rearview mirror, which I always tilt toward her eyes, I can tell who is winning the battle for her attention—my story or the passing scenery out her window. I have learned to begin my stories with a teaser. "Did I ever tell you about the time we saw Houdini's ghost?" "Have I told you about the time Uncle Danny chased me through the house with a fire poker?" "Have I told you about the couple who offered to buy Grandpa for a hundred thousand dollars when he was five years old?" Her eyes fill half the mirror, and I know she's hooked.

To keep her hooked, I have to make my story rich in details. The world I grew up in is completely changed from the world my daughter is growing up in. Even though she will attend the same kindergarten as I did, her experience of that school, of the neighborhood, and of childhood itself will be radically different from mine. Yet she can't get enough of stories about the "old days." To bring her there, I have to season those stories with specific details, like the milk bottles that Ed the Milkman used to leave on our front porch, the candy necklaces we used to buy from the Helms Man, or the feeling of glee we had riding our bikes down a cascade of empty lots now overtaken by homes.

Sophie has also taught me to plant and pay off. Human beings like order, particularly when they are being transported by a story or a piece of music. In a symphony a composer will often introduce a strain of music early on and then return to it later, perhaps at the very end. In storytelling this structuring technique is known as "planting and paying off."

Assigned to write about an accident that happened, one of my students narrated the story of her falling down the stairs. At the time of her fall she was five years old and loved to dress up in her mother's clothes. One day she put on her mom's shiny red high heels and tap-danced around the house to "It's the Hard-Knock Life" from *Annie*. Awkward in a pair of shoes ten years beyond her age, she stumbled at the top of the stairs and bounced all the way down.

Her grandfather, who had been enjoying the album from the safety of his wing chair in the living room, heard Andrea Mc-Ardle's voice skip on the record player and hoisted himself up to investigate. At the bottom of the stairs he discovered his grand-daughter, whimpering in pain and clutching her right ankle, which had swollen so much that she couldn't get the shoe off.

"Get the scissors, Grandpa," she begged. "And cut me out of this thing!"

Her grandfather was old and had the shakes. He came toward her with the scissors open in the ironic shape of a peace sign, both points trembling as they approached the girl's ankle. He managed to wiggle one of the blades between her skin and the shoe, but just then the front door flew open and bumped his arm.

The point of the scissors entered the girl's foot. Her mother, standing on the other side of the door, watched in horror as her cheerful white carpeting got dyed red by her daughter's blood. Eventually both mother and daughter recovered, although the carpet had to be changed.

I had told the class that in their conclusion they should mention a lesson learned from the accident, or a long-term effect. This student wrote, "I didn't give up tap-dancing to *Annie,* but now I'm very careful when I do."

The class liked her story, and so did I. But it didn't quite *land* with us the way it should have (the way *she* probably had, at the foot of the stairs). I thought about why not and then realized that it was my fault: I hadn't taught her to plant and pay off.

After I gave that lesson, the second draft of her story ended like this: *I still tap-dance to* Annie, *but ever since my accident, you can't really hear my heels clicking. I've decided I'm a lot more stable in my own tennis shoes than in my mom's high heels.*

As you read and as you write, keep an eye out for the small details that return later. They make the journey all the more satisfying at its end.

Here is a sample story that I can't tell my daughter yet. It's a traumatizing tale, containing at least three images of extreme violence and one character of evil intent. The gory details would disturb her appetite and her sleep. And the thought that this unspeakable event was perpetrated not by the hand of fate but by the hand of a malevolent human being would discourage her from ever making a play date again, and I'd never get any work done.

You, on the other hand, are tough enough to take it.

TOPIC: WRITE A NARRATIVE ESSAY ABOUT AN ACCIDENT YOU HAD OR AN INJURY YOU RECEIVED. BE SURE TO INCLUDE AS MANY VIVID, DISGUSTING DETAILS AS POSSIBLE.

Head Over Wheels

When I was eleven years old, I rode my bicycle off a cliff. I had been playing tennis at the Mulholland Tennis

Club in Laurel Canyon, a place I visited often during my childhood and where I was favored to win the twelve-and-under singles tournament, scheduled to begin the next day.

On the afternoon of my accident, I had taken a tennis lesson and then gone for swim with my brother Michael. After our swim we changed clothes and packed up our things to go home—my brother on foot and I on my bicycle, which was parked at the top of the long steep driveway beside my father's Vespa.

To a kid in Laurel Canyon, a bicycle was an instrument of freedom and of fun. Mine was a two-wheeler with proud handlebars like the wingspan of a hawk, a reliable foot brake, and thick knobbed wheels that could be ridden off-road and often were. The color of my bike was dark green, and I had named it The Incredible Hulk because it made me feel as invincible as my favorite superhero of the same color and the same name.

But I was not invincible, and neither was my Hulk. As I threw open the clubhouse door, I heard the pop and hiss of a new can of tennis balls being opened on court four, just opposite my bike and my dad's Vespa. There I saw a game of men's doubles about to begin: my father and Norm Greene, M.D., versus two other men. On the court next to them were Norm's son Mitch and a few other junior players, all practicing for the opening round of the next day's tournament.

Whenever my father would ride his Vespa up to the Club, he would strap his tennis racket onto a small metal rack behind the seat. On days when I would be coming up to play, he'd strap mine on, too, so that I could ride my bike safely with both hands on the handlebars. As always before leaving the Club, I slipped my tennis racket under the elastic band on his rack, waved good-bye to him on the court, and swung my leg over the seat of my bike.

My brother had already started walking home. From the top of the long steep hill, I could see him nearing the bottom, where the driveway spills onto Crest View Drive. Just across Crest View is a narrow parking lot built right up to the edge of a cliff. On days when the Club is full, this extra lot absorbs the overflow cars. But today was a Friday, and it was after five o'clock, so the overflow lot was empty.

Eager to catch up to my brother and ride alongside him, I pedaled fast down the first part of the driveway. At the halfway point the driveway levels off for about ten yards before resuming its steep descent. There I realized I was gathering too much speed, so I stepped on the brake. But instead of the firm resistance of the back wheel locking up, I felt the pedals spinning around backward—and the wheels continuing to carry me forward at an uncontrollable speed. In that instant I realized and yelled to my brother: "I'VE GOT NO BRAKES."

My bicycle shot into the street, careening ahead just as a car turned the corner. I heard a wild squeal as the driver swerved to avoid hitting me. The next thing I knew, my front tire slammed into a concrete curb in the overflow lot, and I was hurtling head over wheels off the cliff.

I can't say how long I was in the air, or how many times body and bicycle flipped over, but after what felt like several seconds of slow motion flight, I thudded against the mountain wall, tumbling and sliding down its granite face and then landing in pile of brush fifty feet below.

I couldn't move. The bicycle had pinned me to the ground, and my legs were caught in the brush. I heard my brother's voice calling down to me, "Are you all right?" My mouth was too dry to answer, in part from shock, in part from the dirt and brush I had swallowed. Soon I felt something warm moving down my arm. Glancing down, I saw that it was a trickle of blood flowing from my elbow, where a tiny piece of bone was showing through.

The driver of the car that had almost hit me was the first one down the hill. When he pulled my bicycle off of my leg, it left a row of teeth marks in the shape of the chain, each tiny square colored dark red from the grease mixed with blood. Slowly, he pulled up my shirt. I bent my head forward to look and then quickly looked away: the granite mountain had grated a patch of skin off my chest.

The driver scooped me into his arms and carried me back up the hill. My brother dragged the bent bicycle. A few minutes later I was brought into the lobby at the Club. My father, Dr. Greene, and several others gathered around me. Dr. Greene moved my arm gently, inspected my leg and my chest, and said that nothing seemed broken. My father wrapped me in his tennis jacket and asked Mark, the driver who had hit his brakes just in time, to drive me home.

When my father's Vespa pulled into our driveway, my tennis racket wasn't the only thing strapped to the back. My bicycle was too. My father carried me upstairs and into a warm bath, where he gently cleaned my wounds. Miraculously, I didn't need stitches. I didn't need a cast. I didn't need anything to heal but time.

Norm Greene's son Mitch won the junior singles tournament that year. I had to withdraw because of the accident. Afterward, when I went to congratulate him, he mumbled "thanks" but never looked me in the eye. One of the other players told me that on the day I rode my bicycle off the cliff, he had seen Mitch riding it behind one of the tennis courts and then walking it back to where I had left it, beside my father's Vespa.

I don't know if Mitch tampered with my brakes that day. I do know that one year later, in the fourteen-and-under singles final, I beat him 6–3, 6–2. And after the match, I rode my brand-new bicycle down the long driveway and safely home.

OUTLINE FOR NARRATIVE WRITING OF
ACCIDENT THAT HAPPENED
(GOALS: USE TIME TRANSITION WORDS;
ADD GORY DETAILS; MAKE A CLEAR
BEGINNING, MIDDLE, AND END.)

I.   Introduction. Set the stage and circumstances that led up to accident. Plant a detail to pay off later.

II.   Build suspense leading up to accident. Tip: Use suspense expressions like *I was . . . ing, when all of a sudden . . .* Or *Just then / At that very moment / Before I knew it . . .*

III. The Accident Itself. Narrate each step of the way. Use sensory language to put the reader in the scene.

IV.   The Damage Report. Provide bold, accurate, and disgusting details of the injuries sustained. This is the part that readers love, so be sure to honor them with the gore they deserve.

V.   The Immediate Aftermath. Tell how you were rescued or moved from the scene. Were the paramedics called? Did you limp your way to help? Did a stranger or family member come to your aid? Tell where you were taken—emergency room, doctor's office, first aid office, or home.

VI.   Conclusion—The Long-term Aftermath. What detail did you plant that can pay off here? What scars/memories/lessons were you left with? If you are reading your narrative essay to a class, they will love to see your scars. But you can also have learned a lesson or turned the accident into a success.

Narration is as old as the first campfire around which a story was told. The first time a human being killed a bison, chances are he bragged about it. The first time a child asked why the sun rises in the east, an adult probably made up a story to explain it. The first time a fight broke out between two tribes, their members reported it to the clan. And the first time a boy fell in love with a girl, chances are he told his best friend how they met, and how he felt when they did.

When I was young, we used to tell stories every night around the dinner table. As soon as the food was served and everyone was seated, my father would say, "Well, boys, what did you do in school today?" And one by one my brothers and I would narrate our days. I didn't realize it then, but looking back I can see how that was our campfire time: we were enacting the same ritual that humans have been following since the first time they shared a meal.

Storytelling is such an old tradition that storytellers some-times wonder how they can make their tales unique. Fortunately, the random acts of the universe produce enough newsworthy events that the stories we tell, like the trees we cut down to print them on, are a renewable natural resource. If they weren't, my daughter would have to start taking the bus.

Seven

Thou Shalt Take Pleasure in Thy Pen

IN MY FIRST YEAR OF TEACHING I lost fifteen pounds. On the way to school each morning I would stop by Thee's Continental Bakery at Farmers Market for a cup of coffee and a chocolate chip roll; at recess I would consume a container of full-fat yogurt, a chocolate croissant, and a carton of whole milk; at noon I would rush across the street to Rice Chinese Restaurant and inhale the lunch special, a five-hundred-calorie affair that left my lips freshly glossed; for dinner I would enjoy a pizza—not a slice but the whole pie; and on the way to bed I would stop by the kitchen for a bowl of cereal, comfort food at the end of a long day.

I averaged four thousand calories a day yet lost fifteen pounds in a year. Now I'll tell you the secret behind the Mr. Frank diet: discipline. The only thing you can't have is discipline. During a lesson on subjects and predicates one day, I looked up and saw Karl, a young ruffian in the front row, with pencils sticking out of all five orifices in his head. In trying to stop the avalanche of laughter that ensued, I lost two pounds. The following week another prankster spit water at a girl he had a crush on, and by the time I returned from the bathroom with enough paper towels to dry her off (and enough water to get *him* wet), I had lost three more pounds.

The classroom of a first-year teacher will occasionally receive a surprise visit from the vice-principal, so that the new teacher can be evaluated and counseled if he is doing anything wrong. On the day that Madame Cole, our vice-principal, stepped into my classroom, the first thing she observed was Pablo standing barefoot on the teacher's desk, stomping on the language book and shouting, "I already know what a dependent clause is!"

A high-pitched trill silenced the class. It came from Madame Cole's gold whistle, the one piece of jewelry she wore to school. "Mr. Frank, where is your whistle?" she asked in a tone as starched as her blouse.

The employee manual of our school clearly states that teachers must carry a whistle with them at all times, in order to maintain discipline.

"It's in my car," I confessed.

"Your car?"

"Hanging from the rearview mirror."

"It's supposed to be hanging from your neck."

By the time Pablo was back in his socks, shoes, and seat, I had lost another two pounds.

That night, while scanning the help wanted ads just in case, I had a brilliant idea for disciplining my students: threaten them with a writing topic. The next day, when Pablo touched off a chorus of laughter by leading the boys in a game of Spitball on the Ceiling, I ran to the front of the room and yelled, "If it's not quiet before I finish writing this topic on the board, the whole class has to do it!" Then I furiously scrawled, WRITE A THREE-PAGE ESSAY ON THE CAUSES OF . . .

Pablo's next spitball went splat on his own head. Before continuing the lesson, I informed the now-silent class that I would erase the assignment one word at a time for good behavior—or add to it one word at a time for bad.

The following week I gained one pound.

The threat of writing punishments worked so well that all I had to do was reach for the chalk, and the room would go mute. But one day my discipline tactic backfired in an astonishing way. It was nearing spring break, the students were restless for their vacation, and a fight broke out between Karl and Pablo. The two gladiators were on the floor, ringed by a jeering audience of twenty-one spectators. When the din grew loud enough to land on Madame Cole's desk upstairs, I ran to the board and began punishing: WRITE A THREE-PAGE RES—

The usual curtain of silence fell. But then Pablo had the nerve to peek under it.

"Res . . . what?" he said.

"I didn't write *res*; I wrote *rep,* as in *report.*"

"No, you didn't." He stood up and pointed at the board.

The know-it-all was right. In my haste, I had made a sloppy *p* that resembled an *s.*

"Okay, so it's an *s.* But if you're not all back in your seats and silent, I'll finish the word."

The students darted back to their seats. "Nobody talk!" one homework-fearing girl said. And nobody did . . . for a few seconds.

But then Pablo started to growl: "Rrrrrres!"

I pressed the chalk to the board and raised a menacing eyebrow.

"Rrrrresss!" he persisted.

Impulsively, I added a *t* and an *a* to the word.

"Rrrresta . . . Resta-what, Mr. Frank?"

"Keep talking and you'll find out."

From the back of the room, several students began to growl. From the side, several more: "Rrrresssstttaaa . . ."

"Stop it or else!" I threatened.

More voices joined in. Soon the whole class was growling— *"RESSTTTAAA, RESSSTTTA!"* The room was sounding like a cage, and Zookeeper Cole would blow her whistle at any moment.

Frantically, I finished writing the assignment: WRITE A THREE-PAGE RESTAURANT REVIEW. USE A SIX-PARAGRAPH STRUC- TURE. INTRO., AMBIENCE, SERVICE, CLEANLINESS, FOOD, CONCLU- SION. DON'T FORGET TO DO THE GUM CHECK UNDER YOUR TABLE. DUE MONDAY!

That ought to quiet them down, I thought, tossing the chalk stub into its tray. I turned and saw all twenty-three kids diligently copying the assignment.

On Monday, as my students took their seats for English class, I walked up and down the aisles, a general inspecting his cadets. The room was quiet, the cadets calm. Eerily calm.

"How many people did the punishment?" I asked.

Twenty-three hands went up.

"Good. Take them out. I'm going to collect them."

The compositions came out of the backpacks. Then Pablo raised his hand. "Can I read mine to the class?" he asked.

I hesitated. Karl's hand went up. "Can I read mine too?"

"You want to read your punishments out loud?"

They nodded.

"Anybody else want to?"

The other twenty-one hands stretched high.

My students came up and read, and I sat back and marveled—this was their best work of the year: the reviews were lively, thorough, and entertaining. The reviewers were proud. The punishment had been a prize.

When Madame Cole walked into my classroom a month later, she was met by a profound silence and an intermittent crunching sound. The silence came from the students, who were busy writing and illustrating modern-day myths. The crunching sound came from me: my weight had begun to creep up again, and I was busy eating a rice cake.

I don't have discipline problems anymore, but every now and then my students lose their focus and misbehave. It isn't always their fault. Sometimes it's mine. Sometimes I fail to make a lesson as engaging or as challenging as it ought to be. Fortunately, as soon as the chatter grows loud and the text messages get sent across the room, I return to the chalkboard and think of a new punishment to get us all working again.

I've decided to collect those punishments in this chapter. If you find yourself looking for a reason to misbehave, try one of these . . .

A Restaurant Review

The table was the "right" one socially, the Scotch was from the proper dimpled bottle, the waiter scudded on velvet, other Very Important People nodded and smiled. The slices of salmon were so thin, and the wine came and the rack of lamb, a masterpiece, the headwaiter cool as a surgeon above it.

—M.F.K. FISHER, *"An Alphabet for Gourmets"*

Although I stumbled upon this assignment when I wrote a sloppy *p* on the board, it has endured as one of my students' favorites. I think they enjoy announcing to their parents that the family has to go out to dinner "for homework." I also think they love eating a sumptuous meal and not having to do the dishes.

When you review a restaurant, bring along a discreet pad of paper or notebook. Jot down your impressions, from the greeting you get on the way in to the satisfaction (or indigestion) you feel on your way out. The following outline can help:

OUTLINE FOR RESTAURANT REVIEW
(GOALS: ACHIEVE GOOD DESCRIPTIVE WRITING.
USE A VARIETY OF ADJECTIVES TO DESCRIBE THE
FOOD. DON'T FORGET THE GUM CHECK.)

I.   Introduction. Mention the name of the restaurant, type of cuisine, and general location.

II.   Ambience. Describe the feel of the restaurant, the mood established by its decor, music, type of lighting, and acoustics.

III.   Service. How are you welcomed as a customer here? Is the maître d'/hostess polite? How long do you have to wait for a table? Were reservations accepted? Did you make one? What about the waiter? Was he or she prompt, polite, and accommodating? Or did you feel neglected and harassed?

IV.   Cleanliness. Inspect the rest rooms. Check under your table for pieces of chewed gum. After the meal, reveal that you are writing a review and ask to see the kitchen. But don't do this up front; they will pander to you in an unrealistic way.

V.   Food. This is the heart of your review. Tell what you ordered and what other foods you sampled. Don't go sneaking up to other tables and swiping food off plates. Just taste what your dinner companions have on theirs.

VI.   Conclusion. Give your overall recommendation. Was the food worth the price? Was the evening a pleasant one worth repeating, or is this a restaurant that we should pass by?

At the end of the review, include a fact box with essential information: name of restaurant, address, phone number, type of cuisine, reservations accepted or not, price, and your rating. Your rating can be one to five stars or any other symbols you devise.

Here is a sample restaurant review. It's based on a true story.

GOOD NOURISHING FOOD—AND JUST IN TIME

Located at 8800 West Third Street, Cedars serves wholesome food in a clean, quiet environment. The service is excellent, beginning with the door-to-door shuttle that can be arranged by dialing their twenty-four-hour customer service line. As soon as you are wheeled into the waiting room, you are given a glucose and antibiotic cocktail delivered directly to your bloodstream via a plastic flex tube and small needle.

When your table is ready, you are wheeled to a private room several floors above. My room was on the gastrointestinal wing, and as such it came with a number of highly trained food consultants who helped me decide when and what I should eat. For the first three days I was advised to continue my limited diet of water and the glucose/antibiotic cocktail that I had been given at the bar.

The decor is simple yet attractive. All of the rooms come with a framed art poster, a dry-eraser board, an adjustable bed, and a vinyl-upholstered chair for visitors. In addition there is a wall-mounted color television set to help pass the time between meals. The in-room TV offers traditional daytime and prime-time shows, along with several patient education channels that show documentaries on open-heart surgery, physical therapy, or breast-feeding.

The food perfectly suited my needs. On the morning of my fourth day, I awoke to a glorious sight: a steaming bowl of chicken broth sat on my overbed table, sending its curling aroma into my nose and igniting my long-dead appetite. The soup was accompanied by two saltine crackers wrapped in crinkly plastic. Eagerly I pulled the red tab, freed one of the saltines, and dipped it into the soup. The happy reunion of food with my tongue moved me to tears—the chicken broth was fresh and flavorful and beautifully balanced by the crunch of the saltine.

Several hours later lunch arrived. The waitress was wearing a hair net and plastic booties over her shoes, an outfit that inspired confidence in a disease-free meal. The meal itself, revealed when she pulled a plastic dome from my plate, was a piece of edible art: a small portion of macaroni, no cheese; a piece of dry toast; and for dessert, a glorious rectangle of red Jell-O that trembled when I tapped it with my fork.

My dinner arrived promptly at six o'clock that evening. It consisted of another bowl of chicken broth, the saltines of course, and to my delight, a cluster of steamed broccoli so soft I didn't even need teeth to chew it. Dessert was a Del Monte fruit cocktail in a plastic cup with a foil pull-off lid. It reminded me of the fruit cups my mother used to tuck into my lunch bag when I was in first grade.

If one of the features you look for in a restaurant is cleanliness, you won't be disappointed here. The floors are clean enough to perform surgery on (and indeed they are sometimes used for this purpose). The bathrooms—one for each customer—are cleaned twice daily and come with an assortment of personal hygiene products such as antibacterial soap, a toothbrush and toothpaste, and Vaseline Intensive Care lotion—all included in the price of your meal. The gum check revealed no gum whatsoever. Even a whiff of the air brings the reassuring scent of Lysol disinfectant spray.

My one criticism is the price. My bill for six days, including the shuttle service, came to $24,519.25 (tip included). But for a restaurant experience that caters to your every need, Cedars-Sinai Medical Center is well worth the cost. It just might save your life.

Cedar's Medical Center	Hospital Food
8800 West Third Street	Open 24 Hours
Los Angeles, CA 90048	$$$$$$$$$$
310-855-5000	(most health plans accepted)
	Rating: 5 I.V.'s

Interview Someone at Least Three Times Your Age

"How did the war impact your life?"
"Every way. Every way you can imagine. It took many of my friends. It took away our money. But it gave me my husband."
—CLARA HELFER, *interview with the author*

When I moved into my apartment on North Kings Road, I knew I had a neighbor downstairs. Every morning around six-thirty the muffled sound of a ringing telephone would rise through the carpeting, the bed, and the pillows, finally seeping into my ear. The phone would be answered, and soon a stream of human speech would travel the same path, filling my head with the strange vibrations of a foreign language, I couldn't tell which. Then the phone call would end, and a pair of jack-hammer feet would pound their way across the wooden floor below. Whoever my downstairs neighbor was, he—or she—had a loyal friend, a strong voice, and a brisk, confident stride.

At the end of a week of getting settled, I decided to go downstairs and introduce myself. I pressed the doorbell button, and it got stuck in the on position, producing a long *buzzzzzzz* on the other side of the door. After several minutes of me fran-tically trying to free the button with my short fingernails, the door finally opened, and through a small crack came a long fin-ger with a long nail; the nail picked at the doorbell button, snap-ping it free, and the buzzing stopped.

That finger was attached to a gray hand with brown spots like whorls in a piece of wood; the hand itself, thickly veined yet thin, was attached to a long slender arm in an off-white mohair sleeve; and as finger and hand and arm withdrew, I saw that all three belonged to a woman with white hair, a deeply lined face, and icy blue eyes.

A screen door and, by my first impression, about sixty years stood between us.

"Vhat do you want?" she asked.

"To introduce myself. I'm your new neighbor."

"I know," she said.

We exchanged names—hers was Clara—and I suggested that she call the building manager about the stuck doorbell. She dismissed the suggestion with a wave of her hand. "Those stupid ones don't care about anything up around here." Her accent was European, German I guessed from the way she had said "vhat," but I couldn't be sure.

"It's their responsibility. How long have you lived here?"

"Forty years. I'm an old one. Nobody cares about the old."

The next day I stopped by Clara's apartment to give her my phone number in case she ever needed anything. On my way out I slid on the small braided rug inside her door and nearly fell.

"What'd you do, wax your floors?" I asked.

"Cleaned 'em," she said. "With this."

She pointed to a can of Lemon Pledge furniture polish. In fine print on the back of the can it read, "Not to be used on floors."

"You know it says you're not supposed to use this on floors."

"I can't read that. My eyes aren't so good."

"Clara, it isn't safe. You could trip."

I asked her if I could bring her something from upstairs, and she said, "If you want."

In my previous apartment I had had half a dozen area rugs with antiskid pads underneath. On North Kings Road the bedroom was carpeted, so I had extra rugs—and pads—in storage.

I returned to Clara's apartment with a pad about the size of her welcome rug, and I spread it on the slick lemony floor before replacing her rug.

"There," I said, testing it with a stomp and a skid of my foot. "Now you won't trip."

She stepped onto the rug and tested it with a stomp and a skid of her own.

"How much do I owe you?" she asked.

"For what?"

"The pad."

"Don't be silly. It was just sitting in the closet collecting dust."

She looked at me and then gave an abrupt nod. "All right. Thank you," she said.

Over the next six years I got to know Clara very well. Over coffees, afternoon visits, and occasional brunches in her home or mine, I've learned that her accent is German, her birthplace Switzerland, and the voice on the other end of the line every morning belonged to her older sister overseas. Sadly, the phone stopped ringing two years ago, when Clara's sister died.

During World War II Clara rented a farm outside Berlin. There she led a quiet life, raised chickens, and hid Jews from the Nazis. Among the people whose lives she saved by risking her own was Frederic Helfer, a man who had asked her to dance at a tea dance when she was twenty years old. After the war he asked her to marry him. Clara said yes, and they immigrated to the United States. Frederic died of cancer in 1963, the year I was born. They never had children.

Clara is full of stories—some of them remembrances of

war, others more pleasant, like the time she sneaked into a forest in Germany to watch her father and brother cut down a Christmas tree. She had to take extra-long steps in order to fit her tiny footprints inside theirs.

Since that day nearly eight years ago when I almost fell in her apartment, Clara and I have become good friends. She has been as generous to my family and me as we have been devoted to her. Even the pen with which I'm writing today's pages, an old Parker fountain pen, was a gift from Clara: it used to belong to her husband.

When my family and I move out of North Kings Road, it will be a hard day for Clara—and for me. Soon a new neighbor will move in upstairs. And every day, early in the morning, he or she will be awakened by the muffled sound of a telephone ringing through the carpeting, through the pillow, and into his or her ear.

I know because I'll be on the other end of the line.

You don't need a passport to travel the world. You don't need a time machine to know what it was like during World War II or back in the 1960s. All you need is curiosity, respect for the generations that preceded you, and a grandparent, neighbor, parent, or friend willing to talk about the past.

Questions for Interviewing Someone at Least
Three Times Your Age

When you were my age, what did you do for fun?
Did you ever get into big trouble?

Describe the house you lived in.

Did you have any pets?

What is your fondest memory of your mother? Your
father? Other family members?

What changes in the world made your life easier?

What changes made you sad?

What are you most proud of in your own life?

Do you have any regrets?

Who were your role models or mentors when you were
young?

What advice would you give to my generation?

What advice would you give to your younger self, if you
could speak to her/him?

There are many other questions you will think of on your own, even once the interview has begun. Remember that they are meant to spark a memory. Don't fire them all at once. Give your interviewee a chance to think, to remember, and to respond. And leave room for conversation to develop in between. When you are through, write up the interview as an essay, blending your words with the spoken words of your subject. The essay will be like a photograph, a captured moment when a young person reached out to, and learned from, an old one.

Letters of Complaint

One holiday season my daughter received a litter of Dalmatian puppies. Although they were plastic, the sight of them thrilled her just as much as if they had been real. But her excitement quickly turned to frustration as she tried to open the package.

"Daddy, I can't do it!" she shouted through clenched teeth. And she hurled the package to the floor.

By the time I set the puppies free, my own frustration rivaled hers. I was on the verge of plastic animal abuse, when Sophie stopped me.

"You should write a letter, Daddy."

"A letter? To whom?"

"The people who made the toy. They should know how hard it was to open."

I took her advice:

Consumer Relations
Mattel, Inc.
333 Continental Blvd.
El Segundo, CA 90245-5012

December 21, 2000

Dear Sir or Madam:

We are writing to complain about the packaging of your Disney's 101 Dalmatians Deluxe Collectible Gift Set. The doggies behind the plastic window are so adorable that a three-and-a-half-year-old is eager to break down that window and begin petting the cute puppies at once. However, she soon encounters the cruel barrier of needlessly thick tape and plastic rivets that delay gratification long enough to provoke a near tantrum.

Furthermore, it is too difficult for a toddler to fit the puppies into their proper windows. "Dad, I don't know which ones go in which holes," my daughter keeps repeating while I write this letter. I should inform you that she is an expert puzzle solver and can assemble her Barney floor puzzle in under two minutes.

This is not a letter vilifying you or the Walt Disney Company for contributing to the unwanted Dalmatian population. It is, however, a friendly but firm complaint and request that you change your packaging of this toy and, while we have your attention, of the Barbie dolls as well. Why must the world's most beloved blonde have all of her appendages bound by twisties? This cruel method of restraining her might give little girls—or worse, their brothers—the wrong idea about how to play with dolls. What's more, they frustrate dads-on-duty, who waste precious playtime trying to decide which way to turn.

Please ask your packaging engineers to devise a less twisted method of maintaining Barbie's posture, and a more humane means of caging those black and white spotted puppies.

Yours truly,

Sophie and Daddy.

P.S. "You keep making it too hard for everyone to open them."—Sophie.

The world is filled with injustice, some of it intentional, most of it not. You have two choices when you feel wronged by someone: sulk, or fight back. It's a lot more fun to fight back. And the nice thing about fighting back in a letter is that you take your anger out in a healthy way, through words, and you aim it at the right target instead of something—or someone—you love. (Not to mention the fact that a well-written letter of complaint often provokes an apology, along with a free pair of shoes, coupons for movies, or a discount on your next purchase.)

In order to get a life insurance policy, my wife and I had to undergo a physical evaluation by a nurse from the insurance company. Conveniently, she came to our home with the tools of her trade: a scale, a blood pressure machine, and a syringe. After taking my medical history and my blood pressure, she announced that she would be taking my blood.

I offered her my left arm with the sleeve rolled all the way up to my bicep. She tied a small rubber tube around it, smeared alcohol over the vein she had selected, and inserted the needle. Since I am squeamish about the sight of my own blood, I decided to look out the window during the procedure. Moments later, my view of the trees was altered by a sudden spray of red on the windowpane: the nurse had knocked the needle free, and my blood was squirting everywhere. During her frantic and apologetic search for a cloth, I began composing a letter of complaint in my head. It opened with a legal question: if you bleed to death during a life insurance home medical exam, is your life insured?

The nurse stopped the bleeding and mopped the mess, then ran out of my apartment in tears.

That afternoon a replacement nurse arrived to finish the job. I rolled up my right sleeve all the way to the bicep, looked out the clean window, and prayed. This time I hardly felt the needle go in, and before I knew it, she announced that she was done.

I decided against writing a letter of complaint about the first nurse and instead wrote one of praise about the second. "Nurse Jenny did a first-rate job on our home medical exam," I wrote. "She came to take my blood and left none of it behind."

The next time you encounter injustice, incompetence, or insensitivity, try turning your anger into pleasure: grab your pen. But keep in mind, it's just as much fun to commend as it is to complain.

Satire of Just About Anything

In Ireland in the early eighteenth century, many people were starving to death. The prevailing political opinion was that the government didn't need to act; things would get better by themselves because, after all, individual people are the real wealth of a nation.

Jonathan Swift, author of *Gulliver's Travels,* put forth his solution to the Irish famine in a pamphlet entitled *A Modest Proposal for Preventing the Children of Poor People in Ireland from Being a Burden to their Parents or Country; and for Making them Beneficial to their Publick.* This was Swift's idea: "A young healthy child well nursed is at a year old a most delicious, nourishing, and wholesome food, whether stewed, roasted, baked, or boiled."

In a perverse and very funny way, Swift's *Modest Proposal* does make sense. People are starving; people are having too many children; people should eat their children. Of course, he wasn't serious; he was being satirical. Being *not serious* is the point of satire, a form of writing that criticizes something by making fun of it.

Satire is as old as Aesop's fables and as contemporary as *Saturday Night Live.* Aesop, a slave, wanted to criticize the faults of his captors, but he couldn't do so directly. So he invented the fable, a story in which animals represent humans beings. Twenty-five hundred years later George Orwell followed in Aesop's lead and wrote *Animal Farm,* a satirical fable about the Russian Revolution. Instead of writing a newspaper editorial attacking the hypocrisy of the revolution, Orwell wrote a novel with Lenin and Stalin loosely disguised as the pigs Snowball and Napoleon, and with the Russian citizens portrayed as animals that take over a farm. A newspaper editorial would have been read by many people and then urinated on by their puppies the next day. *Animal Farm* continues to be read and revered a half-century after it was written.

Today satire thrives as a way of poking fun at our politicians. Tune into any episode of *Saturday Night Live,* and you'll see what I mean. Pick up any copy of *National Lampoon* magazine or have a look at the political cartoons in the op-ed section of a good newspaper, and you'll know that satire is alive and well.

A fun variation on satire is parody, which mimics the style of a specific literary work, TV show, or movie in order to make fun of it. In literature *Don Quixote* is a parody of the King Arthur tales. Instead of a handsome, virile, invincible knight in shining armor, Cervantes gives us an aging, bookish, out-of-touch, lovable fool in a cardboard visor. Quixote's lady is not the fair and noble Guinevere but the poor milkmaid Dulcinea.

And instead of attacking monsters or tyrants, Don chases windmills that cut his sword to pieces—his sword, but not his resolve to go on righting the wrongs of a world that he misunderstands.

On television *The Simpsons* parodies shows like *The Waltons* and *Eight Is Enough,* which depict the American family in the warm, cozy, and unrealistic light of perfect civility. In movies you've seen some excellent parodies of long-revered genres. *Blazing Saddles* pokes fun at the western, *Airplane* at the disaster movie, and *Scary Movie* at the horror genre.

Here is a satire I wrote of a letter of recommendation for my colleague Joe. I did two versions of the letter, this one and a straight one. Last year he was hired to teach English at Palos Verdes High School. He still hasn't told me which letter he submitted.

To Whom It May Concern:

I have been an English teacher at the Lycée Français of Los Angeles since 1990. In all my years of teaching I have observed and collaborated with a number of talented teachers, and Joe Harley certainly ranks among the best.

Joe Harley is without a doubt the tallest English teacher we've ever had. On a good shoe day, he stands over six feet three inches high, and all the students look up to him. He is also quite frugal, using only the top half of the chalkboard, which leaves the bottom half clear for students to doodle on. Mr. Harley's moral stature is as tall as his physical one. In fact, one student complained that he refused her bribe of one hundred dollars for an A in his class. "He made me throw in my laptop computer and my cell phone," she protested.

Mr. Harley is also an innovative teacher. In his first year at the Lycée, Joe devised a multicultural approach to literature whereby he proved the superiority of all northern hemisphere cultures over their southern hemisphere counterparts. Students in his class learned to praise the Norse legends, for example, and scoff at the tales of East African tribes. He also saved the students immeasurable time by screening the movie versions of his favorite books: *Animal Farm, Great Expectations,* and *South Park: Longer and Uncut.*

Mr. Harley's commitment to the school has been unbending. Halfway through the year he decided to take a few months off and travel around Europe with the wife of a colleague in the math department. Rather than leave the students without a teacher, Mr. Harley erected a life-size cardboard replica of himself at the front of his classroom, along with a friendly taped message announcing the book, page, and exercise numbers they were to complete each day. Six weeks later, when I entered Mr. Harley's classroom to flip over the tape, my former students were unanimous in their praise of their teacher. "He's never been so animated," they remarked.

If I were looking for a competent, enthusiastic, and tall English teacher, I'd hire Joe Harley in an instant.

Sincerely yours,

Mr. Frank

P.S. We'll be keeping his cardboard effigy, if you don't mind. We need it for summer school.

The targets of the satirist's pen are as unlimited as the politicians on our TV, the preachers on our pulpits, or any other mavens in our midst. (*Maven* is a Yiddish word meaning "know-it-all.") Keep your eyes open for signs of hypocrisy, immorality, or just plain silliness. Then take aim and write any or all of the following suggestions for satire:

A political speech
A policy handbook for professional conduct in the
    classroom
A guide to manners
A guide to dating
The by-laws of a club or organization
A page from the dictionary (include just naughty words)
A page from the driver's handbook
The rules on the bus

If you took any pleasure in the preceding writing topics, turn the page for a few more. They were all originally given as punishments; now I just give them as fun assignments. Somehow over the years my classroom has quieted down. I can't say the change is due to discipline. I don't hand out doughnuts for good behavior or detention slips for bad. I refuse to yell at my students or overwhelm them with piles of homework. I do try to keep them active—actively engaged in thinking, reading, and writing, and in gathering the tools they need to do all three well.

I held on to my whistle, though. It's still hanging from my rearview mirror.

Seventy-five Ways to Wiggle Your Pen: Writing Topics to Last a Year—or a Lifetime

1. Historical Dating Game. If you could go on a date with anyone in history, who would it be? Describe your date, from the greeting to the goodnight kiss.

2. Letter to My Younger Brother or Sister: What to Expect from the Teen Years. For this letter your sibling will be indebted to you for life.

3. I Am the CEO. Pretend you've just been hired as the CEO of a famous company. What improvements would you make? What new products would you launch? And how would you attract the best employees in your field?

4. Clothes Study. Write an essay about the clothes you wear. How do your clothes define and describe you?

5. Politically Incorrect Etiquette. Get your hands on a book of etiquette like *Miss Manners's Guide to Excruciatingly Correct Behavior* or *The Emily Post Book of Etiquette for Young People*. Then try your hand at writing your own funny social guide.

6. My Obit. Write your own obituary (but remember to revise it once a year).

7. Dog's Declaration of Independence. Imagine your dog (or cat) writing a list of grievances about the way your house is run. If your pet were going to sever his or her bond with human beings, what kind of "farewell letter" would he or she write?

8. The "Bottom" of My Life. In *A Midsummer Night's Dream* the annoying big shot Bottom gets turned into an ass. Who is the Bottom of your life—the one person who annoys you the most? How does he or she get under your skin? And if you could transform this person into any animal, what would it be?

9. The Car of the Future. How is technology going to change the way we get around? Write a description of the ultimate automobile in the year 2575.

10. Portrait of a Neighborhood. Write a detailed description of your street and its denizens. Sandra Cisneros wrote a wonderful book, *The House on Mango Street,* with portraits of her neighborhood. Try writing one of your own. When you are older and want to reminisce, this essay will point the way.

11. Literary Metamorphosis. If you could become a character in a book, which one would you like to be? What would you change about the plot of your life?

12. Influence Peddling. What influences our behavior the most—genes, parenting, or peers? Give your take on this controversial issue. Back it up with examples from your life and the lives of your friends.

13. Music Writing. Put on your favorite jazz or classical CD. What images or ideas does it evoke? Listen to the music, and let the ink flow.

14. Look Who's Watching 1. Describe your family from the point of view of the refrigerator/the household pet/the kid next door.

15. Look Who's Watching 2. Describe yourself from the point of view of a homeless person in your neighborhood or on your path to school.

16. Dream Catcher. Describe a significant dream you've had. Try to interpret its signs.

17. Persuasive Writing: Same-Sex Education. Would boys and girls learn better in separate schools?

18. Persuasive Writing: Homework. Are students too stressed out by the homework load, or is it necessary to keep them learning?

19. A Modern-Day Myth. Myths are stories that explain puzzling things about nature or the universe. Try writing your own version of a myth.

20. Last Will and Testament. I know, it's a morbid topic (like topic 6), but it can be handled tastefully—or satirically. How would you like to dispose of your valuables when you no longer need them? You might also include explicit instructions for your own funeral.

21. Ten Things I've Never Noticed. Look around your neighborhood, your home, and your school. Find ten things you never knew were there. Describe them.

22. Review of Just About Anything. Write a review of a book, a movie, a CD, a website, or a car.

23. Take a Poll and Write Up the Results. It could be a poll about politics, social trends, or preferences in pop culture.

24. Campaign Speech. You are running for mayor of your city (or president of your school). Write a campaign speech that touches on the issues about which you are most passionate.

25. Something I Wish I'd Never Seen. Have you ever witnessed something traumatic? Don't lock it away in your subconscious mind. Let it out in words.

26. A New Friend I Made. Write a portrait of a new friend you made. Then tell the story of how you met.

27. Interview Someone at Least Half Your Age. This is a variation of the "Interview Someone at Least Three Times Your Age" topic. Some good interview questions to ask: What is your favorite food? What do you like best about your mommy/daddy/brother/sister/pet? What do you want to be when you grow up? If you could break any rule in your family, what would it be? Do you have an imaginary friend?

28. My Most Embarrassing Moment. You might want to restrict this one to a journal entry, but be honest with yourself. Write about that extremely embarrassing thing you did, how others reacted, and how, with the passage of time, it makes you feel.

29. The Most Beautiful Place on Earth. When you are about to get a tetanus shot, what place would you like to think about to ease the pain? Describe this most beautiful place you know.

30. The Ugliest Place on Earth. A variation on topic 29.

31. The Scariest Place on Earth. This could be a seriously scary place or a humorously scary one. Challenge: describe the same place in two different moods—one eerie, the other humorous.

32. Persuasive Writing: Students Should/Should Not Run the School Cafeteria. Write an editorial for the school paper on whether the students should be in charge of the food.

33. Persuasive Writing: Parents Should/Should Not Be Allowed to Divorce.

34. Anonymous Love Letter. Think of someone you have a crush on. How would you woo him or her? Don't be self-conscious or inhibited about what you write, because you are just doing it as an exercise. Then, when you've put your heart and soul into the letter, take a chance and send it.

35. One Man's Trash Is Another Man's Treasure. Take a morning walk, and pick up three pieces of trash. Invent the story behind each one: what is it, why was it thrown away, and what is the common link among them?

36. A Halloween Tale from the Pumpkin's Point of View.

37. A Family Ritual. What is one thing that your family does every year that makes your family unique?

38. Stream of Consciousness. Blast your random thoughts onto the page for twenty minutes. If you've never tried this, you'll be amazed at how brilliant you can be with no guideline other than write, write, write!

39. The Best Day of My Life. There's got to be one that stands out. Tell about it.

40. The Worst Day of My Life. This is the flip side of topic 39.

41. My Room the Way It Would Be—If They'd Only Let Me. Describe your room the way you would decorate it if your parents gave you free rein.

42. The Perfect Date. You could write this number in the form of a fantasy piece or an advice column.

43. Three New Words the Dictionary Needs. Coin them, and write a petition to get them in.

44. _____s Make the Best Pets. Pick a wild animal that you think would make a wildly fun pet to have. Write an essay in two parts: (1) a scientific section on the animal's physical description, habitat, diet, and mating practices; and (2) an imaginative section on how your life—and house—would change if you brought home such a pet.

45. My Take on God. No matter what religion your family practices, you've probably done some independent thinking about God. Put that independent thinking on paper. You'll be curious to reread it someday.

46. If I Could Be Invisible for a Day. Besides the obvious forays into the bedrooms of the opposite sex, what antics and adventures would you be up to if you could enjoy a day of invisibility?

47. Rulebook for a New Game. Invent a board game, a word game, or a party game. Then write a rulebook for it. Don't forget the catchy title.

48. The Sickest I've Ever Been. Like topic 40, this can be a bit unsettling to write. But we've all been sick and can relate to the misery.

49. Identity Heist: Choose to Be Someone Else and Forge a Diary Entry. This is a fun way to learn about point of view. Pretend you are someone else, and write a diary entry in that person's voice. You could write as a famous person, like the president or an actor, or you could write as someone you know.

50. My Neighborhood—A Hundred Years Ago. Do some research: find old photographs of your neighborhood; speak to old neighbors; look in books on architecture. Then write an essay about your world the way it was. How has the neighborhood changed over the years? How do you think it will change in the years to come?

51. Compare and Contrast Two Members of My Family. This can be a hilarious piece of writing. It forces you to take a close look at the people you know best. What are their habits, likes and dislikes, interests and hobbies? If you are feeling brave, your essay will make good reading at the dinner table.

52. I'm Adept at . . . Write a mild boast of your talents. Come on, everyone has an unusual and praiseworthy talent. It's okay to write about yours.

53. One Thing I'd Change About . . . Myself/My Mom/My Dad/My Sibling.

54. One Thing I'd Never Change About . . . Myself/My Mom/My Dad/My Sibling.

55. Toast of the Party. Most people can't speak in front of a crowd without rambling, stammering, perspiring, and putting the crowd to sleep. A little advance planning, in the form of a *written* toast, can make you the hit of the party.

56. A Time I Surprised Myself. Write about something you accomplished that you didn't think you could do. It could be an athletic or academic triumph. It could be something you built. Or it could be asking someone out on a date.

57. An Extra Day of the Year: What I'd Do. We all know that in a leap year February has an extra day. But what if you looked at a calendar and saw it was January 32? What would you do with this unexpected extra day?

58. The Perfect School. There are many reasons why you can't have everything you want in a school. But there is no reason why you can't imagine everything you want. Maybe the first step to having the perfect school is dreaming it. Try writing this in the form of a brochure that attempts to intrigue prospective students.

59. The Lost Pages. After you've read a book you like, borrow the pen from the author and write a new passage or chapter. Try to craft a new character and setting, and yes, go ahead and imitate the style of the original.

60. Freak of Nature. Write a scientific description of a brand-new species. This is a fun topic for science lovers and future Frankensteins.

61. Silly Constitution. Write a constitution, or plan of government, for the Land of the Silly.

62. Craft of the Cryptographer. Invent a code, and write a letter to a friend in it. You may or may not want to include a few hints for your friend to decipher the letter.

63. Picture the Words. Go to the museum, and park yourself in front of a painting. Describe it in one paragraph, and tell its hidden story in another. What's really behind that Mona Lisa smile?

64. Random Transcription. This may be illegal, so don't publish it. Listen in on strangers' conversations, and write a series of random lines from them. This is a good restaurant activity, especially when the service is slow.

65. Parody of My Favorite TV Show. Write a skit based on your favorite TV show.

66. Recipes to Turn the Stomach. Write some funny recipes that, if someone actually followed them, would produce laughter and indigestion.

67. Letters to My Friends, Idols, and Favorites of Any Kind. People love to get real mail. Write notes to the people whose friendship you treasure, whose books you enjoy, whose designs you feel good in, and whose lives inspire you. Fill their mailboxes with something other than bills.

68. Poems. Become an occasional poet—a poet who writes poems on holidays, birthdays, and anniversaries. Or become an anti-occasional poet—a poet who writes poems whenever he or she feels like it.

69. Advice Column. Pretend you are writing an advice column. Invent problems that your peers are likely to face, and offer intelligent, absurd, sincere, or sadistic advice.

70.   Literary Personals Column. Pretend you are a character from a book you've read. Write a personals ad in which you are trying to get a date.

71.   Travel Essay. Next time your family goes on vacation, take along pen and paper. Take notes on your new (temporary) city or town. Write about its people, its architecture, its food, and/or its culture. How does it differ from home?

72.   Review a Motel or Hotel. Pretend you are an inspector for the auto club, and you are writing a review of a motel or hotel room. Don't forget to check under the bed.

73.   Sound Study. Blindfold yourself, and write a catalog of all the sounds you hear in your backyard, your bedroom, your school, or the car. (Don't do this if you are the driver.) Write down what you hear—and make similes out of the sounds.

74.   Touching Words. Have a friend prepare a banquet of things with different textures. With your eyes blindfolded, touch and describe each item. Make similes out of the descriptions.

75.   A Page from My Autobiography. Your autobiography is going to be five hundred pages long. Write page 499.

Eight

Thou Shalt Not Take Essay Tests in Pain

YOU ARE SITTING IN A HUSHED ROOM surrounded by scores of other students taking the same standardized test. You've zipped or crawled through the math section; you've made it through forty-five minutes of reading comprehension questions and forty-five minutes of vocabulary; your number-two pencil is rapidly turning into a stub; and you could really use a sip of Coke right now. You turn the page of the test booklet, and there before your weary eyes is a word in bold uppercase letters, looming like a roadblock to your future:

ESSAY

Essay? You blink, but the word doesn't go away. You notice another boldfaced horror, this one informing you that the time allotted to write the essay is . . .

30 MINUTES

Thirty minutes! That's one episode of *The Simpsons*! It's how long until the brownies come out of the oven if you like them on the chewy side. It's three slaps of the snooze bar on your clock radio, the time it takes to reach the front of the line for *The Haunted Mansion* at Disneyland, the wait for a table at Benihana or an oil change at Jiffy Lube. When you think of all the things you can do in thirty minutes, writing an essay is nowhere near the list.

But look across the room: there's a girl, her pen dancing across the lines of her test book—*she's* doing it. And look there, a boy who doesn't look any smarter than you, and *he's* already finished an outline, with twenty-five minutes left.

You grab your head in despair. You scratch your scalp and watch the flakes of dandruff snowing down onto your word-less paper. Your ear itches; your rub it and then sniff your finger because—you can't help it—you like the scent of your own earwax.

The exam proctor writes . . .

20 MINUTES

on the board. She is wearing a starched blue suit and too much makeup. You wonder if she has any children at home of test-taking age. Does she roll a chalkboard in front of them at meal-time and write 30 MINUTES on it before announcing, "You may now begin your meal"? You wonder what would happen if you ran up there, grabbed the chalk from her hand, and changed the time remaining to 60 MINUTES. But she'd never let go of the chalk. You can't turn back the time. You can't even slow it down, and soon it's . . .

15 MINUTES

and you realize that now might be a good time to read the question.

TOPIC: "The pen is mightier than the sword."

PROMPT: Write an essay in which you agree or disagree with the topic statement. Support your position with specific examples from personal experience, the experience of others, current events, history, or literature.

You remember a time when you and your brother got in a sword fight with a couple of old tennis rackets in the garage. At one point he knocked your racket out of your hand and was about to deliver the fatal thrust to your chest, when you swerved out of the way, whipped out a pen from your jeans pocket, and poked him in the leg with it. He dropped his racket and ran blabbering into the house. You were punished, but you had won the fight. Your pen had been mightier than his sword.

Double-checking the prompt, you see that personal experience is allowed, so you decide to write about the sword fight with your brother. You are going to agree that the pen *is* mightier than the sword, and you start thinking of examples to support your position:

1. The pen can be concealed.
2. People are more likely to be carrying a pen than a sword.
3. A pen is filled with ink, which could poison someone.
4. Pens are cheaper.

Now you're feeling comfortable enough to write your essay. But just as you're brushing aside the pile of dandruff, the lady in the starched blue suit says, "Put your pencils down." You look up at the board and see . . .

0 MINUTES

Game over.

What happened to you in this hypothetical situation happens to many students in real situations all the time. Faced with having to write under the pressure of a ticking clock, they panic, they daydream, they freeze. And before they've even lifted their pencil, it's time to put it down.

It isn't just while you're in school that you will have to write under pressure. Journalists work under deadlines. Salesmen have to devise their pitches on the plane—or sometimes on the spot. What office assistant hasn't heard the command, "On my desk in twenty minutes!" (I'm referring to a memo) from an impatient boss? The fundamentals of writing a speedy response to a prompt, any prompt, apply as much to the secretary or the CEO as to the student. The task can be an intimidating challenge. It doesn't have to be.

An Ounce of Prevention

There is a proverb that states, "An ounce of prevention is worth a pound of cure." It means that it is better to head off a disaster beforehand than deal with it after. It is better to replace the batteries in your flashlight every six months than to wait until there's an earthquake to see if they have any juice left. (I speak from experience.) It is better to spend $75 a year to have your automatic transmission serviced than $1,200 on a new one when yours breaks down. (I speak from experience.) It is better to visit the doctor for an annual checkup than to wait until you're dead of a heart attack. (I speak from fear.)

When it comes to taking essay tests, that ounce of prevention isn't optional; without it there is no cure. If you've absorbed the first seven Pen Commandments, then you've already prevented many of the disasters that can occur during those fateful thirty minutes. An awareness that your writing will be read by a human being, a thrifty style, and the ability to write clear, correctly punctuated sentences will help distinguish your essay from most others. A solid command of structure will also make your essay stand out, as will mastery of narrative, descriptive, and persuasive writing. And if you take pleasure in your pen, the essay you craft will surely rise to the top of the heap, a sunflower among shrubs.

But even a faithful keeper of the Pen Commandments can

feel intimidated by writing under pressure. In this chapter we are going to erase your fear.

When I told my wife I was writing a chapter on essay tests, she asked me when I thought we should start preparing our daughter to take them.

"It's already too late."

"How can it be too late? She can't even hold a pencil."

"Yeah, but she can hold a thought. She can even hold two thoughts at the same time, and that's the first skill she'll need on an essay test. We should've been preparing her in the womb."

My wife thought I was kidding and walked out of the room, so I'll have to finish our conversation here, with you. What I would have explained is that the ability to hold two thoughts at a time is the key to figurative thinking, which makes connections between two apparently dissimilar things that actually have something in common. When my daughter was two and a half, she looked out the window one day and saw a crew of tree trimmers giving a buzz cut to the ficus on our corner. Two men were up in a cherry picker with their gas-powered saws, gnawing through the thick branches and letting them crunch to the ground. "Look, Daddy," she said. "They're just like beavers." She had made her first simile, and I knew exactly how it had come to her. The week before we had watched *Lady and the Tramp,* and she remembered the scene in which Tramp tricks a beaver into biting off Lady's muzzle. In the movie there is a shot of the beaver cutting down trees to make a dam. Outside our window men were enacting a similar scene. Her brain made the link.

Very young children make these links all the time. Their minds are primed for figurative thinking, because everything is so new to them. Like an enormous page of connect-the-dots, the world to a two-year-old is an elaborate maze, and with each new connection they see a wider piece of the puzzle. Somewhere between three and thirteen, many of us start losing this capacity to wonder. We get jaded, blasé, or cynical, and men trimming trees aren't beavers anymore; they're just background noise.

The more links you can make between your own experience and the experience of others, the deeper will be your understanding of the world. The more similarities you can see between historical events and current events, the wiser you will be. And the more parallels you can notice between stories in literature and struggles in life, the more perceptive you will be.

That depth of understanding, wisdom, and perception is what the readers of your essay are looking for. Consider the proverb *The pen is mightier than the sword*. It can be taken two ways, literally and figuratively (although it's meant to be taken just one way). Its literal meaning is that a pen can beat a sword in an actual fight. Its figurative meaning is that the pen can create things—through writing—that will defeat even the strongest sword. The pen belongs to the philosopher, the sword to the warrior. Martin Luther King, Jr., used a pen to write his "I Have a Dream" speech. James Earl Ray used a "sword" (in that case, a gun) to shoot King dead. Which was mightier? Long after the speaker was killed, his speech is still heard. The Civil Rights Act of 1965, which that speech inspired into existence, is still the law of the land.

The reason you see proverbs on standardized tests is that they make good essay topics. According to *The Random House Dictionary of America's Popular Proverbs and Sayings,* "proverbs are the collective wisdom of all nations, of all ages, of all times. A proverb typically expresses a commonplace thought in a succinct, often metaphorical way." By "metaphorical" the author means the opposite of literal. In other words, if you miss the metaphor, you'll miss the meaning.

Now, you may be thinking, "How can I have enough experience to agree or disagree with the collective wisdom of all nations, of all ages, of all times?" Good question. The answer is, you aren't expected to possess all that wisdom; you are expected only to have an opinion about it—and to support your opinion with examples from your experience, your reading, or your studies.

Might makes right.
Haste makes waste.
Actions speak louder than words.
Neither a borrower nor a lender be.
People who live in glass houses shouldn't throw stones.

What do you think about these proverbs? Do you agree or disagree? Do you think they are true or false? What is your take on the "collective wisdom of all ages"? And most important, how are you going to back it up?

Not all essay questions will be based on proverbs. Some will ask you to write about a role model, a life-changing experience, or a trend in our society today. The one thing all of the essay topics will have in common, however, is that they will all be designed to provoke an opinion.

No one can tell you what your opinion is. But there *is* someone who can help you deliver that opinion. His name is Mr. Smith.

Mr. Smith's Rules for Safe Driving

In high school, I took many fascinating courses, but the one that left the deepest impression on me was driver's education. On rainy days when we couldn't joyride in the Dodge Darts provided by the L.A. Unified School District, our instructor would screen *Mr. Smith's Five-Point Method of Safe Driving,* a twenty-minute training film. With his trademark 1950s short hair, boxy black glasses, and bow tie, Mr. Smith was a good-natured geek who drove as conservatively as he dressed. The most attractive woman in the world could be sunbathing nude by the side of the road, and Mr. Smith wouldn't even swerve. A child's ball could come rolling into his lane, and Mr. Smith wouldn't even skid as he stopped a safe distance from the child who came running after it. He was a man of five principles, which he shared with us as he drove through a quiet suburban neighborhood:

1. Get the big picture.
2. Aim high in steering.
3. Keep your eyes moving.
4. Make sure they see you.
5. Leave yourself an out.

These aren't just driving tips; they are kernels of wisdom, a guide to a happy and fulfilled life. What's more, Mr. Smith's tips on safe driving apply as much to writing as they do to the road.

1. *Get the Big Picture*

When you sit behind the wheel of a car, it is important to take in the whole road, not just the narrow view through your windshield. The same is true when you sit down to write an essay. And in order to get the "big picture," you first have to . . .

READ THE
DIRECTIONS

When it comes to directions, people fall into one of two categories: (1) can't be bothered; (2) always take the time. Think of the last new electronic device or toy you received. Did you rip open the box, plug it in, and turn it on? Or did you meticulously lay out all the parts, read the instructions, and fill out the warranty card *before* playing with it? If you're like me, your tendency is to plunge right in and read the instructions only if something doesn't work. If you are like my wife, you read and understand the directions before breaking the inner seal on the parts.

There is a wonderful proverb that people like me should have branded on our foreheads: HASTE MAKES WASTE. In my rush to play with my new electronic device or toy, I often overlook some key point in the directions. I forget to load the printer drivers, for instance, when I buy a new computer. Or I'm so eager to wear my new sweatshirt that I toss it into the washing machine without reading the care instructions on the back of the tag. As a result of this tendency toward haste, I am forbidden to do either the laundry in our home or the routine maintenance on our computers. I am also extremely qualified to give advice on the importance of reading directions.

Here are sample directions from an SAT practice test:

Read the following topic carefully. Take a few minutes to think about the topic and organize your thoughts before you begin writing. Be sure that your handwriting is legible and that you stay within the lines and margins.

TOPIC: Imagination is more important than knowledge.

ASSIGNMENT: Do you agree or disagree with the topic statement? Support your position with one or two specific examples from personal experience, the experience of others, current events, history, or literature.

Now, a hasty person like me might zip through the directions and start writing ten support paragraphs, five in agreement with the topic statement and five in disagreement. For each side of the issue, I would write one paragraph based on my personal experience, one on the experience of others, one on a current event, one on history, and one on literature. Just as I'd be racking my brain for an example from history, the proctor would announce, "Put your pencils down." I would be caught halfway through the essay I had intended to write, with no time to proof-read and no conclusion to satisfy my reader—all because I hadn't read the directions carefully and failed to notice a tiny, two-letter word.

It says *or*! Agree *or* disagree. Support your position with one *or* two specific examples. The examples should come from personal experience, the experience of others, current events, history, *or* literature. In other words, *narrow the scope of your essay*. After all, you've only got . . .

30 MINUTES

Besides reading the directions, another way you can get the big picture is to expand your life experience. As a student, you are caught in that in-between world that is part childhood and part adulthood. The poet William Wordsworth wrote a famous line about the relationship between a young person and the adult he will grow up to be: "The child is father of the man." It seems unnatural (and illegal) for a child to be a father. But Wordsworth's line, like all good poetry, shouldn't be taken literally. In a figurative sense, it means that just by being alive, all young people are automatically pregnant with the grown-up version of themselves. And during this pregnancy, which has a gestation period of twenty-five to thirty years, everything you observe, experience, read, and hear is going to nourish the developing adult within.

The formal essays that you write, like an ultrasound image of a fetus, can give a preview of that developing adult. If your life is filled mostly with school, family, video games, television, and music, then those will be the raw materials you draw on for specific examples in your writing. There is nothing wrong with watching television, seeing movies, listening to rap music, and playing video games. In fact, some contact with popular culture is an essential building block of your social life. (It's also fun.)

But if pop culture is all you're ever exposed to, how will your essay be unique? Most student essays use personal experience to support a thesis statement. Unless you've had an extraordinary experience that taught you a clear life lesson related to the topic, your examples may seem commonplace to the reader. Why not get the big picture and stand out from the crowd?

You could start with the newspaper. If your parents don't get a daily newspaper, ask them to subscribe. If they're allergic to newsprint or prefer getting their news from TV or the Internet, then find a job delivering papers. (You can read one at the end of your route.) If you have trouble waking up at five A.M., ask a neighbor who subscribes to save the paper for you every day. If your neighbors are toilet training a new puppy, remind them that puppies learn faster on the classifieds, and ask them to keep the other sections for you.

Now many of you are probably thinking, "I don't have the time to read the newspaper. The articles are too long." I had the same objections in high school, when George Schoenman would tell us that he never closed his eyes at the end of a day without having read every word of the paper.

"You don't expect us to do that," we would plead.

"No, you guys are too busy," he'd say. "But it wouldn't kill you to read everything on the front page."

Yes, it would have. And it certainly would kill today's homework-battered high schoolers. So here's a good compromise: don't read *all* the articles on the front page. Don't even read half of them. Read one. Just one, including its continuation on another page. Total elapsed time for this task? Fifteen minutes— five at breakfast, five in the bathroom after breakfast, and five in the car or bus to school.

What will happen if you follow this advice? You might get carsick, but your expanded vocabulary and larger point of view will be worth it. Instead of saying, "Dad, I think I'm about to barf on your leather seats," you'll say, "Dad, I think I'm about to regurgitate on your leather seats." When meeting a girl from Brazil, instead of saying, "¿Hola, cómo estás?" you'll know to say in Portuguese, "Oi, como vai?" And when your SAT scores arrive in the mail, a full fifty points higher on account of your daily dose of the newspaper, if your parents decide to reward you with a trip to Papua New Guinea, you won't have to ask where it is.

Another excellent way to expand your experience is to watch something you don't usually watch on TV. Instead of Saturday-morning cartoons, try the Discovery Channel. Instead of sit-coms, watch documentaries. Tune into the story of Eleanor Roosevelt, Gandhi, or Napolean on *Biography*. *Wheel of Fortune* might teach you a thing or two about spelling, and *Jeopardy* might tuck a few new facts into your brain, but you'll learn much more from a half hour of the History Channel than from a week's worth of game shows. Remember: you are the mother or father of the woman or man within. Your future self is in the womb. Feed him well.

You can make similar choices in what you read. I hate the expression "reading for pleasure," because it implies that all other reading is for pain. Yes, *A Series of Unfortunate Events* is entertaining, *Harry Potter* is a triumph, and even *Sweet Valley Twins*, at a certain age, is addictive. And while I would much rather see my students reading anything than nothing, I would also like to see them reading the kinds of books that J. K. Rowling read when she was young, books that stretch their minds.

When I look back on my own childhood, I see huge holes in my reading. As an adult, I have had to go back and read classics like *Treasure Island, Call of the Wild, Robinson Crusoe, 1001 Arabian Nights,* and *20,000 Leagues Under the Sea.* I still haven't read *Little Women, Black Beauty,* or the entire *Lord of the Rings.* I feel like I'm still catching up to my students, and it gets harder and harder now to make the time.

Classic is a funny word. Mr. Morelock, one of the sports teachers at my school, has a 1936 Model T Ford. Whenever he drives his "classic" to school, the students all gather around and ask to go for a ride. But when I bring my book bag to school and start pulling out "classics," everybody runs. They run so fast, I don't get a chance to tell them my definition of a classic, which is a book you can take off your grandmother's shelf and read with as much pleasure and interest as she did fifty years ago. Classics are classics because generation after generation they have something relevant to say. In fact, most classics can take you for a far more thrilling ride than Mr. Morelock's sputtering Model T.

Classics create a common bond between you and the readers of your essay. When the instructions tell you to give examples from "literature," they don't mean *Animorphs*. The more references you can make to books that are read by all generations, the more likely you are to make a positive impression on the college graduate reading your essay.

Another way to broaden your experience is to *pay attention in school*. I know, sometimes it's impossible. A fifth-period class on the Middle Ages can be pure anesthesia. But if you'll take a few sips of Coke after lunch, you might stay awake long enough to learn something. Many students burn their history notes at the end of the year. These aren't the ones who score above 1500 on the SAT. If you look at your class notes only twice—once as you're writing them and once again the night before a quiz— look again: these notes are a gold mine of big-picture references to include in your essays. Whether it's a proverb, a political slogan, or a passage from the Bible, the topic for your essay can always be supported with specific references to history.

Think about your last history lesson. Can you find anything in your class notes that would help you to agree or disagree with these quotations?

Neglect breeds discontent.
Those who forget the past are condemned to repeat it.
No pain, no gain.

If you've studied the Boston Tea Party, you have a clear example of how neglect breeds discontent. If you've studied Stalinist Russia (and read *Animal Farm*), you'll see how those who forget the past are condemned to repeat it. If you've studied the civil rights movement in America, you'll be able to support the statement, *No pain, no gain*. But in order to support these statements effectively with historical events, you have to know the events well; you have to pull your notes out of the fire and read them again.

Are you lucky enough to have a grandparent nearby? If so, you have a living witness to history, someone who can give you an insider's view of the very period you might be studying in school. My Great-uncle Moe lived to be ninety-nine years old. As a boy, he had been taught Civil War songs by veterans who had visited his school. Ninety years later Moe sang to me:

> Bring the good ole bugle boys, we'll have another song
> Sing it like we used to sing it fifty thousand strong
> While we were marching to Georgia
> Hurrah, hurrah, we'll sing the jubilee
> Hurrah, hurrah, for the land that makes us free
> Sherman's dashing Yankee boys will have another song
> While we are marching to Georgia.

At ninety-nine Moe had lived through the turn of the century, both world wars, the Depression, the Korean War, and the Vietnam War. He had voted in twenty presidential elections, seen the first movie ever made, heard the first radio broadcast, typed on the first electric typewriter—and on the first laptop. He was a wellspring of knowledge for me, and I was lucky to know him.

Some of you may have grandparents who were at Normandy or parents who marched with Martin Luther King, Jr.

You may have neighbors who lived through World War II in Europe, who witnessed the Cultural Revolution in China, or who recall the Cuban Missile Crisis. You may even have some former flower children living at home. The older people among us shouldn't be sitting in front of their televisions answering game-show questions. They should be answering *your* questions about their lives, about our history.

Every year I give my students an assignment to interview someone at least three times their age. They prepare a list of twenty questions designed to provoke stories from the past. Last year in reading the transcript of one of the interviews, I saw the following exchange:

STUDENT: Grandma, you never told me you were a nurse in World War II.
GRANDMA: Darling, you never asked.

Start asking. Start listening. And start remembering. In order to get the big picture, you have to widen your point of view.

2. *Aim High in Steering*

When Mr. Smith told us to aim high in steering, he meant that we should see the road far ahead. By aiming high, we would keep our car on a steady path—making no sudden movements, no last-minute swerves.

When writing an essay, you can avoid sudden movements and last-minute swerves by planning ahead. By reading these pages, you are already aiming high: long before you turn onto the road of a pressure essay test, you are learning what to expect.

And once you do set out to write an essay, you can keep your aim high by writing a short outline during the first few minutes of the test. Remember that you are not expected to write *War and Peace* or *Harry Potter and the Goblet of Fire* in thirty minutes. You *are* expected to respond to the prompt with two *or* three clearly stated and well-supported paragraphs. Your outline for these paragraphs should be *brief*.

Aiming high in steering can also help you keep perspective. Many students get nervous when taking formal essay tests. Your anxiety can be so strong, it releases a brain-altering hormone, like a fog, that freezes the ideas in your brain and the ink in your pen. If you have a tendency to panic during a test, take a moment to breathe. And take another moment to remember that your life does not depend on this one exam.

The road ahead stretches far beyond a single essay. Just past the next curve is another chance, and beyond that another, and soon you'll come to a long stretch of open highway, your whole life, and someday while cruising that highway, you'll glance in the rearview mirror, and that essay you froze on, or that boss who barked at you for being late with a memo, will be completely out of sight.

3. *Keep Your Eyes Moving*

For the purpose of advising you on how to take an essay test, I have to make a slight change to Mr. Smith's instruction here. If I let it stand, you might misinterpret and keep your eyes moving around the room. This misunderstanding will result in disaster for us both. You will waste time with those wandering eyes, and I will be sued for contributing to the delinquency of a minor. When the exam proctor accuses you of cheating, you will defend yourself by saying, "Mr. Frank told me to keep my eyes moving," and then we'll both be thrown in jail.

So let's change the advice to read, *Keep your pen moving*. In other words, don't waste time. Writing a thirty-minute essay has to be a swift action. If you are going to feel nervous, tentative, anxious, or afraid, do it now, in the safety of your own room, but recognize that once the thirty minutes begin to tick, for every panic impulse you give in to, you will lose irreplaceable time.

If you do hit writer's block during the exam, pause and breathe. While the essay is important, it is not worth dying for. And sometimes a few calming deep breaths can alleviate the anxiety in your way.

Also remember that the advance preparation you are doing now—and will continue to do as the test date approaches—will eliminate 90 percent of the fear caused by these exams. The outline you wrote when you aimed high in steering will keep you on track. Trust the outline. Stick to it. If it was created with enough thought, it will guide you all the way through.

4. *Make Sure They See You*

Mr. Smith made his training film long before road rage. He believed that a "friendly toot of the horn" was all you needed to avoid a collision with another driver who wasn't paying attention. If Mrs. Jones, for example, were backing out of her driveway but relying on her rearview mirror instead of a direct sight line, he would give her a "friendly toot of the horn" to notify her that he was nearby. In the training film Mrs. Jones responds with a courteous wave, and Mr. Smith sails on by. Nowadays she would point anything at him from a middle finger to a machine gun.

Tooting your own horn during an essay test is a lot safer than tooting it on the open road. Suppose your essay is at the bottom of the pile, or your reader is barely awake. How will you get his or her attention? In order to make sure they see you, you have to do something to distinguish your essay from the thousands of other essays being written and read.

The first step is to make sure that your handwriting is legible. On my sixth-grade report card from Wonderland Avenue School, I received a D in handwriting. In seventh grade the first elective I took was typing. I figured that the future belonged to the keyboard—or at any rate, mine did. But guess what? You still have to write your standardized essay by hand. If I had to take an in-class essay test now, I would probably fail on account of my atrocious handwriting. If I slow down, I can make my writing quite neat, but at that monk's pace my thirty minutes would elapse before I'd finished the introduction.

Once you are confident that your handwriting is clear, you can begin to think about the more substantial ways to make sure they see you. First among them is to grab the reader's attention with a bold topic sentence or provocative rhetorical question. Then let your reader know he or she is in safe hands by supporting each of your points with specific—and explicit—examples.

Suppose, for instance, that you are agreeing with the proverb *No pain, no gain*. You've chosen the civil rights movement to support your topic sentence. Look at the difference between vague and concrete support:

VAGUE

The proverb "No pain, no gain" is clearly supported by the civil rights movement. Many citizens suffered, but their suffering helped bring about a change. If it weren't for the hardships experienced by both the leaders and the followers of the civil rights movement, no new laws would have been passed to stop discrimination. Therefore, it is obvious that the pain they went through was worth the gain they got in the end.

CONCRETE

The proverb "No pain, no gain" is clearly supported by the civil rights movement in the United States during the late 1950s and early 1960s. Following the philosophy of civil disobedience espoused by Gandhi, the activists in the civil rights movement deliberately exposed themselves to painful situations in order to challenge unfair laws. For refusing to give up her seat to a white man on a Montgomery, Alabama, bus, Rosa Parks was arrested and sent to jail. This personal sacrifice led to an even greater sacrifice by her fellow black citizens of Montgomery, as they boycotted the city's buses in protest of segregation. They experienced the pain of walking to work instead of taking the bus, and some of them had to face the pain of unemployment after losing jobs because they arrived late to work. However, these pains were finally healed by the passage of the Civil Rights

Act of 1965, an important gain for the black citizens of Montgomery and for all minorities in the United States.

The difference between the two paragraphs, besides length, lies in the specific examples of pain (Rosa Parks and the Montgomery, Alabama, bus boycott) of the second paragraph, as opposed to the general ones ("many citizens suffered") of the first. Also, the second paragraph makes a specific link between the pain and the gain ("these pains were finally healed by the passage of the Civil Rights Act of 1965"), whereas the first refers to the general "no new laws would have been passed."

The essay writing you do on a standardized test is like the persuasive writing you learned in Chapter 6. Like a lawyer before a judge, you need to present specific evidence to support your case. If you do, you'll win the case—and win over the reader.

Another effective way to stand out is to memorize a few quotations from novels, plays, or poems that you might be able to include in your essay. Before I took the Advanced Placement test in English, George Schoenman advised me to memorize a few passages from Shakespeare. "Nothing impresses an exam grader more than quotes from the Bard," he said. Among the speeches I learned was one from *Macbeth*:

Out, out, brief candle
Life's but a walking shadow,
A poor player that struts and frets its hour upon
    the stage
And then is heard no more.
'Tis a tale, told by an idiot,

Full of sound and fury,
Signifying nothing.

The essay question was about titles. I had to choose a literary work from a list and write about the significance of its title. Lucky for me, *The Sound and the Fury* was on the list, and I had memorized the very passage that had inspired its title. With the quote from *Macbeth* clearly in my head, I was able to include it in my essay on Faulkner's novel. I am convinced that this advance preparation helped me pass the exam.

Now, let's be reasonable. Even if you are in high school, you may not have read enough literature yet to know what is worth memorizing. But just as you should read *one* newspaper article a day, try memorizing *one* Shakespeare passage or *one* stanza of a famous poem each week. The benefits of learning famous lines by heart go beyond the cryptlike room of a standardized test. For one thing, memorizing poetry is a kind of calisthenics for the mind and may ward off Alzheimer's disease. For another, the poetry you learn will keep you company in the long lines at the supermarket, the DMV, or Disneyland.

You can also get the reader's attention by using challenging vocabulary words in your essay. Here again your school notes can come in handy and should not be burned. Make flash cards of the vocabulary words from your English class, along with the ones you meet in newspaper and magazine articles. Make a pact with yourself to learn three new words a day. Don't just memorize them, either. Master them. Use them in a practice sentence. Walk into that essay with an army of words at your command, and you will capture the attention of even the weariest reader.

Finally, remember that you're entitled to a title. Very few writers of the pressure essay include a title at the top of their composition. A good title, like a friendly toot of the horn, can make a wonderful first impression.

5. *Leave Yourself an Out*

Mr. Smith's last tip for safe driving is to leave yourself an out. On the road this advice translates to the three-second rule—when the car in front of you passes a fixed point, you should be able to count three full seconds before your car reaches the same point. It also refers to leaving yourself a safe maneuver to avoid an accident. If the car behind you is tailgating, change lanes and let it pass. If a large truck is boxing you in, slow down or speed up—whichever is necessary to find a stretch of open highway.

Leaving yourself an out on an essay test means writing an effective conclusion. Your conclusion should restate your topic sentence—but not in the same words. If my topic sentence was, "The proverb 'No pain, no gain' is clearly supported by the events of the civil rights movement in the United States," then my conclusion should *not* be, "In conclusion, the civil rights movement of the United States clearly supports the proverb 'No pain, no gain.'" That would be a violation of Pen Commandment 1, Thou Shalt Honor Thy Reader, because it would be repeating a sentence still audible in the reader's head.

A more effective conclusion would be to reaffirm the proverb's relationship to the civil rights movement but put a spin on the topic, a ripple in the reader's mind that he or she will ponder long after you get your test result in the mail. How do you come up with such a spin? I can't answer that question with a rule or a method; I can only say that a conclusion will suggest itself at the end of a good essay, and if it doesn't, don't worry. You can always just paraphrase (but not literally repeat) in succinct, clear language the main idea your essay has proved. A statement like "Although the civil rights movement was marked by much sacrifice and suffering, it did lead to significant gains for all citizens" would be a sufficient conclusion.

A stronger one would include an *image* that captures the spirit and substance of the movement. The image of an Alabama bus today, for example, with multicolored faces in its windows, might give us a conclusion like this:

> If Rosa Parks were to step onto a Montgomery bus today, she could take a seat wherever she wanted. At eighty-nine years old, she would probably sit in front, in the seats reserved for the elderly and the handicapped. Sitting beside her there might be a white woman, an Asian man, or the very police officer who arrested her forty-four years ago. She would look out the window, and her face would fill the glass, one square in the mosaic of America, a work of art crafted from much pain, yet reflecting even greater gain.

Mr. Smith's three-second rule applies to the end of your essay too. But I would substitute three *minutes* for seconds. Part of leaving yourself an out is leaving yourself a few minutes to proofread. Read over your essay once for logic and a second time for mechanics. On the logic pass, make sure that all of your sentences make sense. On the mechanics pass, fix your fragments and stop your run-ons. If you've repeated a word, neatly line it out and replace it with a synonym. If you've misspelled a word or misplaced a comma, make the correction. For every error that you catch on your way out, you'll give your reader a more hospitable, gentle farewell.

Not long ago, my wife and I ran into a friend of hers with her two kids, one in fourth grade and the other in eighth. I noticed that Craig, the eighth grader, was looking somewhat glum, so I asked him how he was.

"Miserable."

"How can you be miserable?" I said. "You don't have any pimples."

"I'm taking the SAT in three years."

"Three years is a long way off. Why fret over it now?"

"They're adding an essay."

I remembered reading an article about the College Board's new policy on the SAT. They were adding an essay because they felt it was the most important—and till then overlooked—measure of a student's aptitude.

"I'm terrified of essays," Craig confessed.

"And they don't give him much help at school," his mother added.

"Well, what kind of essay do you have to write?" I asked.

"A fast one. About an important experience I've had. Or a proverb. I don't even know what a proverb is."

I explained proverbs to him, using *An ounce of prevention is worth a pound of cure* as an example.

"I'm going to need a pound of prevention," he said, slouching away.

As I watched him go, I realized that his pain was my gain. This anxious, haggard eighth grader had given me a new idea for a chapter in my book.

"Better hurry up and write it," my wife said. "Three years goes by fast."

Well, I *have* written this chapter in time for Craig to read it and, I hope, benefit from it. If it helps him, I'll give it to my daughter to read as soon as she learns how. After all, *The early bird catches the worm.*

Nine

Thou Shalt Overcome Writer's Block

MY DAUGHTER IS SO GOOD AT OPENING string cheese that she has become the mother hen of her lunch table at preschool.

"Hey, Sophie, will you open this?" Nick asks when he encounters the familiar snack in his Spiderman lunch box. Sophie grabs the string cheese, feels around for the invisible weak spot, and tears. She pulls back the taut plastic skin as swiftly as if it were a banana peel.

Samantha waits her turn, Marty his. As soon as all the string cheeses are opened and safely in the mouths of her classmates, Sophie, who doesn't even like string cheese, yanks the foil lid off her strawberry Yumster and eats.

For many people, facing a blank piece of paper is like staring down a stick of string cheese: they know there's a secret place where you are supposed to tear; they know that if they can just find this place and rip, their writing will flow; yet they spend hours trying to locate the hidden zipper, and often their search ends in desperation, in hunger.

This is a chapter about writer's block, a common affliction that all writers succumb to at some point and that most suffer through alone. The symptoms are easy to spot. Those who have the disease drink more coffee than usual and get less sleep; they exchange fewer pleasantries with strangers and offer more criticism of family and friends; they answer the phone in a voice that makes you wish you hadn't called; and they rebuff your sincere *What's wrong?* with a sharp *Nothing, I'm writing,* even though they're not. If you encounter someone in this miserable condition, the only sensible advice to follow is to avoid him or her at all costs. But the advice I give is to call back. Offer to help.

In the first part of this chapter, we'll look at six methods for curing the disease. In the second part, I'll present case studies of people I know who have struggled with familiar yet burdensome writing tasks, the kinds of "assignments" that stump you not only in school but all through life.

Writer's Block—Suggestions

Find Your Cave

Some writers can't write in public. Others can't write at home. Some need a window to look out. Others prefer a blank wall. Billy Wilder wrote in the bathtub, Marcel Proust in bed. Richard Ford writes wherever he is—on a bus, aboard a plane, or in a hotel room. "Like Emerson's giant," he has said, "I take my desk with me." It doesn't matter where you write, as long as you find the place with the fewest distractions for you. Your cave could be a library, silent and studious. It could be a café rumbling with anonymous noise. It could be a garden, a rooftop, or a favorite step on the stairs.

My own cave—call it an office, if you like euphemisms—is a three-by-five foot closet off our living room. For a desk I've converted a pressboard shoe shelf and set it on top of a waist-high ledge. There isn't room for a chair, so I do most of my writing on foot, or I open up an old wooden stepladder and rest my haunches there. The closet has a lovely diamond-shaped stained glass window, but it doesn't open. With the door closed I have more than enough privacy but not quite enough air. So for health reasons I have to limit my writing stints to an hour. Anything longer, and I'll be asphyxiated by my own sighs.

By creating a sacred space in which to write, you give the act of writing a higher rank than, say, the act of eating (which you probably do in the car, on the couch, and in class) or the act of sleeping (which you probably do in the car, on the couch, and in class), or the act of daydreaming (which you probably do in the car, on the couch, and in class). The first step in defeating writer's block, then, is to give yourself what Virginia Woolf called a room of one's own, a place where you are expected, and you expect yourself, to write.

Phone a Friend

Sometimes you will come out of your cave empty-handed. Don't despair. One of the best cures for writer's block is conversation. You call a friend and announce that you're about to jump, and it's up to him to talk you down. Your friend then asks a series of questions: "What are you trying to say? Can you put it in plain words? Can you collect all your thoughts under one big idea? What's your most important point?" You answer simply, directly, and truthfully. As the conversation continues, your friend will ask more specific questions about your project. Now here's the key to getting you off the ledge: your friend needs to take notes on everything you say. Later he will fax you the transcribed conversation, and as you pull the fax from the machine, you'll behold the bones of your essay, letter, synopsis, or speech. Of course, these will just be the fragments; now that you're unblocked, you will have to flesh them out, shape, smooth, and polish them into a workable draft. But it's better for the *essay* to be in pieces than for the writer to be.

Put Up with Imperfection

Writing is rewriting. This remark has been made by many authors, so I don't know whom to credit for it. But it's true. Other than essays written under the gun, most of the writing you do is done ahead of time. Joyce Carol Oates writes a book and then puts it away for a year before rewriting it. This separation gives her enough distance from the first draft to fall out of love with it and into the unbiased editorial gaze that a second draft demands. (Of course, she gets to work right away on her next manuscript.) You may not have a year's cooling-off time; often a day will do, a day for your words to rest on the page, a day for your mind to rest too. Then when you return to your poem, essay, love letter, or chapter, its flaws will reveal themselves and surrender without a fight.

Knowing that you'll have a chance—an obligation, really—
to rewrite also frees you from the perfectionism that holds many
writers back. It's a first draft. Let it be flawed. It's easier to have
something to fix than nothing at all.

Set Your Compass

In one of Isaac Bashevis Singer's funniest stories, "When
Shlemiel Went to Warsaw," the wanderlustful Shlemiel resolves
to leave his village of Chelm and visit Warsaw. Since there is a
Warsaw Street in Chelm, he naturally concludes it will lead him
to straight to the big city, and he sets out on foot.

The sun goes down, Shlemiel grows weary, and he decides
to rest for the night along the road. But how will he remember
which direction he was headed before he fell asleep? In a stroke
of navigational genius, Shlemiel takes off his shoes and points
the toes in the direction he was going. That way he'll be sure to
pick up in the morning where he left off.

Unaware that he is being watched by a mischievous spy,
Shlemiel goes to sleep. The prankster then sneaks up and turns
his shoes around, in the opposite direction. This is not a story to
be read while you are eating. The comedy that ensues when the
sun comes up and Shlemiel puts on those redirected shoes will
send your lunch flying.

Besides being hilarious, "When Shlemiel Went to Warsaw"
carries a sound message for blocked writers: don't get caught
with your compass pointed the wrong way. If Shlemiel had used
a pen instead of a pair of shoes, he could have written himself a
note: *Go this way,* followed by an arrow straight to Warsaw.

If your writing task takes more than a day to finish, end each session with the first sentence or a brief outline of the next day's work. End on a beginning, not on an end. That way when you return to your task, you will have already given yourself at least a walking start, and you won't be a Shlemiel—you'll make it to the real Warsaw.

Alter Your State of Mind
(Disclaimer: I Don't Mean Take Drugs!)

When I used to play competitive tennis, I would sometimes hit a slump as frustrating as any bout of writer's block. My backhands would wobble, my overheads would land on the next court, and my serves would fizzle into the net. The only thing that got me out of my rut was to spend a few days watching tennis, not playing it. Seeing other players, *better* players, practice their craft inspired me to return to mine. And often when I did take up my racket again, it felt lighter, more obedient, because I had learned a tip or two just by observing someone else.

For a writer in a slump, that someone else is any other writer whose work you admire. Take a book from the shelf and read. Read to replenish your supply of words, of ideas. Read to forget your problem. Or read just for fun. Then when you return to writing, your mind will be rested, and often your problem will be solved.

Charles Dickens used to walk his way out of writer's block. For three or four hours, and sometimes for an entire night, he would wander the streets of London, and he would think. Then he would head back to his desk and let his thoughts come out on paper. A screenwriter I know shoots baskets when he gets stuck. You can tell by the relentless bouncing of the ball that he's suffering through a thorny plot point (usually in the second act). But after a while the ball rolls off the court, and his keyboard gets clicking again. My brother alters his state of mind in the pools of New York, Rome, and Astoria, Oregon. For forty-five minutes a day he swims up and down a narrow lane in a smooth, almost placid rhythm, as steady as a pen across paper. By the time he emerges from the water, he tells me, he has a clear vision of his next writing session. I've often thought he should leave his laptop at the edge of the pool so that he won't lose time drying off.

You can also do the unthinkable: you can nap. I can't admit this to my wife, because she assumes that when the door to my office is closed, I'm working. And I usually am. But every now and then, because I'm either stuck or simply exhausted, a wave of drowsiness overtakes me. There isn't room in my office to stretch out, so I take my naps like a horse, standing up. They don't last long—Seven Minutes in Heaven is all—but when I wake up, miraculously, my subconscious mind has solved the problem, and the words flow again. Picasso cured his painter's block in a similar way. He would nap holding a silver spoon, and as soon as he fell into a deep sleep, his hand would open, the spoon would clatter to the floor, and he would be jarred awake, ready to work.

My naps have led me to another insight about writer's block: it's best to write by the first light of day. In that margin between sleeping and waking you'll find your most fertile state of mind. Take only the essential detours from bed to desk. (The bathroom is essential; the kitchen is not, unless for coffee.) This time of day is like the time just after a bath, or just after birth, when you are closest to your subconscious. As Auden advised, "Work first and wash afterwards."

Adopt a Ritual

Asked in an interview how he finds inspiration for his songs, James Taylor said, "I don't find the songs; they find me. I just strum my guitar and wait for a lyric to come." His answer reveals an important truth about writing: while its purpose is practical—to communicate—its process is often mystical—to receive.

The ancient Greeks recognized the mystical in all creative acts. They invented the nine muses, goddesses who would inspire poets, musicians, artists, and authors. People with writer's block often utter complaints like "My muse is having an affair" or "She's left me an orphan" or "I'm still waiting for my muse."

I have always prided myself on my rational thinking. In the 1970s, when an astrology craze swept through my junior high, I was such a devout nonbeliever that I would lie about my birthday just to mess with the self-proclaimed astrologists who insisted on doing my chart.

"When's your birthday?" they would ask.

"June second," I'd say, a full month and a half shy of the truth.

"Gemini. And what time were you born?"

"Four A.M." (It was really four P.M.)

A week later some acne-skinned seer would produce an elaborate map of my personality—my strengths and weaknesses as a human being; my tastes in food, music, art, and girls; my aptitudes for certain subjects in school and my struggles in others. Of course, the chart was pure rubbish, and I would just nod, enjoying the inside joke between me and my rational self.

But when I compared the results of my chart to the personality traits of my older brother, whose date and time of birth I had given in place of my own, I gulped: it was all true, even down to the detail that he was happily dating a moonchild. And though I'm still an emphatic nonbeliever in all things superstitious, I have to admit there are *some* things that the rational mind just can't see.

One is the face of a muse. So like James Taylor, I recommend embracing the mystical part of writing by adopting a ritual. Ernest Hemingway couldn't write unless he had twenty pencils lined up in front of him, all perfectly sharpened. He was terrified of losing his rhythm while sharpening a pencil, so he got them ready in advance. Toni Morrison has to have a cup of coffee before dawn. "It must be dark—and then I drink the coffee and watch the light come." John Cheever believed that his muse would come to him only in his primal state of being, so he adopted a strict dress code for his working hours: he would don a suit and tie to leave the apartment, and then, once he was downstairs in the boiler room of the building, he'd take off his clothes and write in the buff. A friend of mine writes on an old Underwood manual typewriter that he bought from an antique dealer in Oakland, California. He claims the machine is possessed by the soul of its previous owner, whom he believes to have been Jack London. "Jack London died when he was only forty," my friend says. "But he keeps on writing through me." (I don't have the heart to tell my friend that Jack London's type-writer was a Remington.)

My own ritual is a quirky bit of superstition that I haven't even told my wife about. But I don't mind telling you. I write my first drafts longhand, on clean white unlined paper, and the pen I use has to be a gift from one of my students, a family member, or a friend. It's sort of like the Japanese tradition of never refill-ing your own cup of sake—you always wait for your sushi part-ner to pour. By writing with a pen that someone else has given me, I am waiting, appreciatively, for my muse to pour.

Writer's Block—Case Studies (The Specific Task Is in Parentheses)

My Mother (Sympathy Note)

Whenever my parents' circle of friends gets redrawn a little smaller, I'm always the first to hear.

"Honey, I have bad news. Alice Blayden died."

"Oh, Mom, I'm so sorry. Was it expected?"

"Is it ever?"

She sighs into the phone. And suddenly her sadness gives way to stress. "Listen, do you have a minute? I'm writing a note to Charlie."

"Gee, Mom, I was just getting to work on my—"

"Oh, come on, *Mister* Frank. You can write *The Pen Com-*

mandments, but you can't help your own mother with a condolence note?"

She's guilted me into taking a new sheet of white paper. "Okay, what do you want to say?"

"What can I say? I didn't really like her that much."

"'Dear Charlie, I'm glad it was your wife who died and not you.' How's that?"

"You think this is funny? The funeral's in two days. I am not going to the funeral unless the sympathy note's in the mail."

So I do what a good son does. I help my mother out of her writer's block.

"All right, what have you written so far?"

"'Dear Charlie, Marty and I were so . . .'"

"Devastated?"

"Not really."

"How about saddened?"

"Okay, saddened. 'Marty and I were so saddened . . .'"

"'. . . to hear about Alice's death.'"

"Spit-spit. I'm not using that word."

"Mom, it's what happened to her. It's what happens to us all, if we live long enough."

"Can't we just say, 'saddened to hear about Alice'?"

"Yes. He'll know what you mean."

"Okay. Now I'll write, 'If there's anything we can do, don't hesitate to call.'"

"That's a condolence cliché, Mom. You don't want to write that."

"What do I want to write?"

"Something specific. Something meaningful."

"Didn't you say you have work to do?"

"Yes, but now that you've got me started—"

"Darling, I can write the rest. Really."

"Mom, the note's not supposed to make you feel better. It's just supposed to make you *feel*."

On the other end of the line, silence.

So I go on. "Who was Alice? What did she mean to you?"

"We didn't have that much in common. She always had to order a second cup of coffee when we were trying to make an eight o'clock movie. She used to criticize Charlie in front of his friends."

"In all their years of marriage, did she ever do anything nice for him?"

"She nursed him through two bypasses. He was a lousy patient."

"And in all your years of friendship, did she ever do anything nice for you?"

"She visited me every day for a week after Grandma died. She was always good to you kids."

"See? She wasn't all bad, Mom. Nobody is."

There is a long pause on the other end of the line. "Did you know that I dated Charlie before I married your father?"

"No, I didn't."

"He liked Alice better."

"That must've been hard for you, Mom."

"It ended up being the right choice. For both of us."

"Listen, I have to go. I hear Sophie waking up from her nap."

"You can't hang up. We haven't finished writing the note yet."

"Yes, we have. Wait five minutes. I'll send you a fax of everything you said."

My mother attended Alice's funeral, and the next day she received a call from Charlie. "Your note meant so much to me," he said. "You were one of Alice's favorite people. Mine too."

My mother never knew.

My Wife (Thank-you Notes)

Soon after my wife and I were married, we became extremely intimate—with the UPS man. I never thought I would be so glad to see a man in a brown shirt marching up to my doorstep, but march he did, several times a week, bearing abundant gifts. We showed our gratitude to the UPS man by buying stock in his company. We showed it to our wedding guests by writing each one a fond and thoughtful thank-you note.

One morning, on the occasion of the UPS man's third appearance on our doorstep, I carried a heavy item upstairs and plunked it down on the dining room table. "This one's for you, honey." The return address on the box was from the east, where most of my wife's family still lives.

"Oh, God," I heard her exclaim as soon as she had sifted through the pile of Styrofoam packing material. "What are we going to do with this?"

She held up a large framed painting of a sunset in the Grand Canyon. The colors were bold: all lavenders and pinks, with a fiery orange ball sinking behind the canyon rim. Predominately a landscape, it did pay homage to a handful of desert critters: a jackrabbit, a pair of sidewinder snakes, and in the background a proud hawk searching for prey. It was so vivid that I could smell the dusty, fecal scent of an Arizona trail, and I had a sudden urge to swing my leg over the back of a mule.

We stood there for a long moment, anesthetized: this was the ugliest piece of art we had ever seen, in a museum, in a motel room, or by the side of the road.

"Will you write this one, please?" my wife begged. She was referring to our agreement that I would write the thank-you notes to my side of the family and she would write them to hers.

"Sorry, honey, they're your relatives."

First she affixed the stamp. Next she addressed the envelope. Then she took out a crisp white thank-you card and began to think.

At 12:15 I brought her lunch.

At 4:00 I made her a cup of coffee.

At 6:15 I went shopping.

At 7:30 I served her dinner.

My wife loves French toast for breakfast, and when I set some before her the next morning, she still hadn't finished writing the note.

"Syrup?"

She shook her head. "Help."

What's a new husband to do? I gave in and sat down.

It didn't take me long to come up with the perfect thank-you note. "Dear _____ and _____, we are so appreciative of the painting you sent. In a young marriage such as ours, it is essential to know up front what each person's taste is. The moment we opened your gift, the newly married Mr. and Mrs. Frank knew we had a long and happy life ahead, for we simultaneously leaned over the glass and vomited."

"Is it too soon to get a divorce?" she asked.

"That's actually a good idea. We'd have to return all the gifts—including this one."

"I'll let you keep it," she said, "as part of the settlement."

We considered for a moment. Then I got another inspiration. "Dear _____ and _____, thank you for the lovely painting you sent us. It does more than illuminate our home; it shows us in the clearest light that we should have registered for the things we want."

She flung a piece of French toast at me. Meanwhile, the UPS man kept on arriving with more gifts, and as the pile of unopened presents grew, I realized that drastic measures were needed.

"We'll lie," I said.

"What?"

"Dear _____ and _____, choosing a piece of art for someone can be risky, but this time the risk has found its reward. We've been searching for an aesthetic style that we can agree on, and your painting has shown us the way. It will hang over our mantel, close to our wedding picture. We hope to have you as guests in our home, to see how lovely it looks on our wall."

"What if they come out to California?"

"We'll treat the painting like a tax return: keep it in the garage for five years. After that there's no danger of being audited."

I used to believe that grown-ups wrote *No gifts, please* on the invitations to their parties because they had outgrown the need for toys, clothes, and electronic gadgets. I used to think they had entered the age of spiritualism and abandoned the slavish materialism of youth. But the truth is, they don't want to write the thank-you notes. They consider them a chore.

I like to think of them as an opportunity. Forget about the stuff—there's too much clutter in the world anyway. And even if the gift was given from a sense of obligation, the thank-you note that acknowledges it can mean something more. When it came to my half of the list, I would write my thank-you notes mostly about the people who sent the gift, with a line or two about the gift itself. These were friends of my parents, friends of mine, or members of the family. Some traveled a long way to our wedding. A few wouldn't live long enough to attend the next family event.

When my wife realized that the couple who sent us the painting probably wouldn't return to California in the next five years, she found she did have something to say. Not about the painting—it could remain in the garage and they'd never know—but about the relatives. This is what she wrote:

Dear _____ and _____,

When we were planning the wedding, my mom kept saying, "Julie, we have to cut the list down. It's too many people." And I kept saying, "Mom, it's the people that count, not the place. We'll get married on the beach, in the backyard, or at the airport if we have to. But I want everyone to come."

And you came. You came all the way from New York. I am thrilled that your picture will always be in our album, and that your painting will be in our home. It was so nice of you to choose a piece of art for us.

Love, Julie.

I've got to hand it to my wife; that was an artful thank-you note. Notice that she emphasized the human element: the relatives came such a long way to be at our wedding. Notice also that she didn't lie: *Your painting will be in our home.* The verb *be* is, in this case, the perfect noncommittal word. *Hang* would imply on a wall. *Adorn* would suggest a decorative function. But *be* is safe. It's particularly safe because as soon as we move into our new house, the painting will move into our garage and still be "in our home." (The house plan calls for an *attached* garage.)

Faced with writing a thank-you note for a gift she didn't like, how did my wife get over her writer's block? She found something truthful to express. She realized it's not the gift that counts. It's not even the thought. It's the people.

Peter the Procrastinator (Essay About Literature)

A former student of mine once called for help on an essay he was writing for his honors English class. It was a peaceful Sunday night in my house—I had just fallen asleep with my daughter—when the phone jolted me from a dream.

"Mr. Frank, it's Peter. Um, sorry to call so late, but I've got this essay to write."

"When's it due?" I mumbled into the phone.

"Tomorrow."

I pressed the light button on my watch; a dusky blue light broke the bad news: ten-fifteen P.M.

"I see."

"I didn't wake you, did I?"

Peter is fifteen years old. He won't know what it's like to be a parent on a Sunday night for many years. But since I remember what it was like to be a student on one, I said, "No, Peter, just give me a minute to go to my office."

My office is lit by a naked bulb above my head. I reached up and yanked the chain. The harsh light woke me the rest of the way up.

"So tell me what the topic is."

"We have to write about the supernatural in *Wuthering Heights*."

I did an instant recall: Heathcliff, Cathy, moors, passion, social class, ghosts.

"Did you finish the book?"

"Yeah, this morning."

"And what have you been doing all day?"

"I started to work on the essay, but then I found this great Internet site for Pictionary."

"You've been online gaming?"

"I didn't plan to. But I was staring at the screen for so long, and I couldn't think of anything to write, so I kind of clicked on the AOL icon, and one link led to another."

"Peter, didn't I teach you to find your cave, to do your writing someplace with no distractions?"

"I know, but there's something about the Internet. It's hard to resist."

"Do you have a typewriter?"

"We threw it away."

"How about a pen and a piece of paper?"

"Yeah."

"Get them. And unplug the computer until your first draft gets written by hand."

"Okay."

"Now, let's talk about the book. Did you notice any ghosts?"

"Cathy's a ghost. She haunts Heathcliff on the moors."

"Do you remember what page that's on?"

"I marked it."

"What else did you mark?"

"In Chapter Twenty-nine Heathcliff makes the sexton open up Cathy's coffin. She's been dead a long time, but when he looks at her face, it hasn't decomposed at all. It looks almost alive. That was cool."

"Does the gravedigger notice this too?"

"It isn't clear. It's up to the reader to decide."

"What else?"

"Her spirit appears to Lockwood in a dream. He sees her trying to get in through the window, and he tries to stop her but ends up cutting his finger on some glass."

"Is there blood there in the morning?"

"No."

"So is it real?"

"Maybe. Maybe not."

"Talk about the setting. Anything stand out?"

"The moors. They're eerie. Very damp, foggy, and in the fog you can't see what's really there, but you can see what's not. In the end the villagers say they saw Heathcliff's ghost wandering in the fog."

"But still there's no proof, is there?"

"I don't think there needs to be."

"What do you mean?"

"The ghosts don't have to be real. They're like memories. Heathcliff and Cathy are memories too. They're characters in a story. And the way it's told is kind of supernatural. Nelly is telling their story to Lockwood, who is telling it to his diary, which is telling it to us. So he gets to know Heathcliff and Cathy as ghosts, really, because they're not there in the room; and we get to know them as ghosts, because we're just reading about them."

"They're all in our head. I like that, Peter."

"And if you think about it, it's kind of true about all stories."

"How?"

"Well, all stories are ghost stories, because characters aren't real. They're only there in words. I found this great quote about the name Catherine showing up in lots of places around Wuthering Heights. Here it is. 'A glare of white letters, as vivid as spectres. The air swarmed with "Catherines."' The letters. The word. The ghost. And the character. It's all the same."

"I think you'll be able to write this now. I'll fax you what you said—I've been taking notes."

"Oh, thanks, Mr. Frank. That's great. That'll really help."

Peter stayed up until four-thirty hand-writing his essay on *Wuthering Heights*. He wasn't blocked anymore—he took the notes from our conversation and expanded them, revised them, and organized them into a rough draft. But he was worried that the rough draft had too many little mistakes, so he asked for an extension and polished the essay before handing it in.

The next day he called to thank me. "I didn't know I had it in me," he said.

"You've always got it in you, Peter. It's just a matter of getting it out."

My Younger Self (The Application Essay)

The College Application Essay is a nasty beast that starts taunting students in the summer before twelfth grade. Imagine all the hairballs you've ever pulled from the shower drain rolled into one gleeful and mischievous creature; now imagine this creature taunting, "You're going to have to write me, you're going to have to write me," and you'll have a clear picture of what we're up against.

Why is it so difficult to sum up who you are in a "brief, well-organized essay of five hundred words or less"? First, because you have to know who you are. Most writers of the College Application Essay are still figuring that one out. Then there is the problem of your autobiography. While the "facts of life" are thrilling, the facts of a single life—the "David Copperfield crap," as Holden Caulfield would say—are often too boring for the College Application Essay.

A complete understanding of an individual is difficult, perhaps impossible, to achieve from an essay of this length, but I will try to communicate who I am by providing the reader with a brief overview of the milestones of my life.

Sleeping yet? Now I have a confession to make: the author of that particular dose of anesthesia is none other than *moi*, Mr. Frank. It was the opening to my College Application Essay, and I would like to take this opportunity, here and in print, to apologize to the poor souls who suffered through that drivel. To those who accepted me in spite of my essay, I hope I have redeemed myself.

The milestones of my life. They were more like pebbles. Was I born with a rare congenital disease that I had to overcome in order to speak? Was I a war orphan from Vietnam? Was the Frank family a clan of refugees from Cuba or El Salvador? Or did I have a basically good childhood with elements of mischief, friendship, heartbreak, and happiness?

What about extracurricular activities? Since middle school you've been cajoled, bribed, bullied, and begged to join the fencing team; edit the yearbook; run for school president; run for city council; do a summer course at the Cordon Bleu institute; write, direct, and star in the school play; or volunteer at your local shelter for retired racing dogs. You've lived in terror of those large rectangles on the college application, the ones where you "list any extracurricular activities that might be of interest to the Admissions Committee." Long before you even fill out an application, and in some cases while you're still in diapers, they stare at you like panes of thin ice: fill them up with a solid bridge of your accomplishments, or risk drowning in your own cold mediocrity.

How do *you* spend your hours out of school?

a.   Hanging out with friends;

b.   Sleeping;

c.   Engaging in activities you can't confess to even in an anonymous multiple choice survey; or

d.   Ladling soup at the homeless shelter

If you answered (d) ladling soup at the homeless shelter, you might have an extracurricular worth writing an essay about. But if, like most people, you answered (a), (b), or (c), you don't.

What should you write, then? Since a "complete understanding of an individual" really is impossible to get from a brief essay, it's okay to give a partial one. Often you will be prompted to describe "a personal experience that had a significant impact on your life." Notice that it doesn't say, "a significant experience that had a personal impact on your life." It's a personal experience, no matter how small, that had a significant impact.

If I could travel back in time to the fall of my senior year at Fairfax High, I would rip up the Application Essay I wrote and urge myself to start over.

"But I don't know what to write," the young Mr. Frank might confide in the old.

"You could write about the time the '64 Buick—a car that had been handed down from one brother to the next—caught on fire."

"We saved it, remember?"

"Of course I remember."

"Danny and I were in a big fight when it happened. But when Dad threatened to scrap the car, we said, 'No, we'll find a way to fix it.'

"We went to Pep Boys and bought three rolls of electrical tape, brand-new wire, new hoses, spark plugs, a new air filter. We didn't know much about cars, but we learned. Then we spent the rest of the day replacing all the burnt parts. We worked on the driveway until it got dark. We worked in the garage until it got light again. And when we were finished, the old '64 started right up. It ran for another twenty thousand miles after that."

"We fixed more than just a car that day."

"But is that what they want to read?"

"Better that than how you played on the tennis team."

"What else could I write about?"

"How about the time we had to put Mannix to sleep?"

"He was old. He was blind. He was pooping in the house."

"He even pooped in the car on the way to the vet. One last bit of mischief, one last mess."

"He was in pain."

"Remember how we went in with him? We talked to him and rubbed his tummy as Dr. Miller put the needle in."

"He said it was the right thing to do. He said we should do it for humans who suffer too."

"When we got home, and Dad saw just the collar and the leash in our hands, he started to cry. He turned around and ran upstairs so we wouldn't see him."

"The Admissions Committee's not going to care about putting the family dog down, are they?"

"He was our childhood dog. That's a big thing. It was the first time we'd seen our father cry. That's even bigger."

There are books you can buy that give advice on how to write the College Application Essay. They include actual essays written by students who were accepted at Ivy League schools. But before you rush out to paraphrase one of those successful essays, you should know that the members of the Admissions Committee get the updated edition of those books every year as Christmas presents. They'd rather read something original, something true.

Instead, why not alter—or expand—your state of mind by reading some essays by masters of the form? Read the classic essayists like Montaigne, Emerson, and Thoreau. Read contemporary ones like Russell Baker, Anna Quindlen, Philip Lopate, M.F.K. Fisher, and Bailey White. You'll find that a personal essay is never just about the writer. What makes it personal is that it is relevant and interesting to any person who reads it.

One essay I read five years ago has remained with me ever since. It was written by a girl whose sister had anorexia. She wrote about the impact the illness had on her family and on herself. "I finally realized that I couldn't make my sister better," she wrote. "And if I didn't stop trying, I would make myself sick." Not everyone has a sister with an emotional disease, but we've all had a sibling or parent or friend whom we wanted to help but couldn't.

In "The American Scholar" Emerson wrote: "It is remarkable, the character of the pleasure we derive from the best books. They impress us with the conviction that one nature wrote and the same one reads." His words are just as true for the best essays—college admission or any other kind. The reader of that essay longs for you to be authentic. Your goal isn't to say, "Hey, look at me! Look at the fascinating life I've lived, all the accomplishments I've done!" It's to say simply, honestly, "Look at the world for a moment through my eyes; here's something I've noticed, or experienced, or felt. Maybe you have too."

Anyone Who Gives One (A Speech)

"The world is divided into two kinds of people: the optimist, who sees the glass as half-full, and the pessimist, who sees it as half-empty." Thus began a graduation speech I once had to endure for a fully empty forty-five minutes. The world, as anyone who's lived in it knows, is divided into many more than these two types. There's the wine connoisseur, who wants to know what's in the glass; the skeptic, who wants to know who poured; the germophobe, who wants to know who's been drinking from it; the fashion hound, who wants to know the brand of lipstick staining the rim; the bargain hunter, who has a set of the same glasses at home and wants to know what you paid for it; the ADD sufferer, who wants to blow bubbles in the glass; and the nihilist, who'd like to hurl it against the wall.

Of all the responses to the proverbial glass, I'm partial to that of the nihilist: this is one glass that is better shattered and swept into the trash than continually rewashed and reused by lazy speechwriters.

The best graduation speech I ever heard was given by a stand-in valedictorian when the real one got strep throat. He could have just read her speech, but it wasn't his style, so he made up his own. This was a high school senior whose mom's bumper sticker read: "My son is an honor student." But the words "honor student" were crossed out and below them was written "awesome skateboarder."

He was an awesome speaker too. Reed got up in front of his classmates, teachers, administrators, family, and friends, and he talked about the bike path at Venice Beach. Speechwriting 101 teaches that you have about thirty seconds to grab an audience's

attention. You can do this with an anecdote, a quote, a provocative question, or a shocking statement. Reed began with a confession: "Now that I've got a diploma, I can tell you that I
ditched a lot of afternoon classes so I could hang out at the
beach."

"We know!" his teachers shouted back. The ice was broken.
Trust was established between speaker and audience. And the
tone was set: this wasn't going to be your cliché-cluttered "the
future's not ours to see, but it is ours to make" kind of speech.

Speechwriting 101 teaches that the middle of your speech
should develop one or two themes with several specific points to
support them. Reed's first theme was the real world, the one far
away from our school, that he observed at Venice Beach. "So
many different kinds of people go by on their bikes, blades, or
boards," he said. "So many different kinds shoot hoops down
there, or try to make a buck, or beg for food." Then he talked
about three specific people he had observed: a Rollerblader who
never got off his cell phone; a spray-paint artist; and the Bubble
Lady, a homeless woman who blew bubbles for her dog to chase.

He had us all laughing as he delivered his predictions about
who in his class would be doing what on that boardwalk in ten
years. This was the part of the speech where he clearly knew his
audience, mentioned them by name, and made specific observa-
tions that we all felt were true: Matt, headed for business school,
would try to turn the boardwalk into a mall; Becky, the silent
valedictorian who had fought for recycling bins on campus,
would organize a human chain to stop him; Luis, our very own
Keith Haring, would be working alongside the spray-paint artist;
and Maria, the clumsiest girl in the class, would knock the cell

phone guy off his 'blades—and they'd probably fall in love. "As for me," Reed said, "I'll be blowing bubbles with the homeless lady and her dog—unless I improve my attendance record in college."

Speechwriting 101 teaches that you should end by tying it all together and perhaps leaving the audience with something to think about. Reed told the simple truths he had learned from ditching school. He didn't exhort anyone to "go forth and change the world." He just said, "Find your own place in it. Pick a major you're really into, not the one your dad says is practical. Get a job you love. Buy a hybrid if you're worried about the environment. Or better yet, ride a skateboard. And marry someone who's totally on your side." Here he looked at Wendy, the star of the school play whom we all knew he had a crush on. "Someone like me."

Her answer: "Ask me again at the ten-year reunion."

Talking to a crowd . . . you'll have to do it some time in your life. Whether you run for office, make a sales pitch, testify in court, speak to the PTA, roast a best friend at his wedding, or remember him at his funeral, life has a way of putting you on a stage.

Step up with pride—and a speech in hand. Use a clear structure. Find the right tone for the occasion. Avoid clichés and trust specifics. Do what Reed did: be yourself. At the end of his speech, there wasn't just one glass, half-empty or half-full. We all had our own. And we had the feeling, even those of us who were decades out of high school, that we could fill our glass any way we wanted.

———

Recently I was the working parent at preschool. I got to play chase with the kids, help them build forts out of wooden blocks, lead them in the cleanup song, and read them a story at lunchtime. I also got to bring the snack.

I had heard my wife describe how Sophie was an ace at opening everyone's string cheese, so I made it the centerpiece of what I served, along with organic apples and Wheat Thins. I wanted to see the mother hen in action.

When we delivered the snack tray to Sophie's table, Nick asked her to open his string cheese. But this time she refused. "You have to learn how to open it by yourself, Nick," she said. "Someday I'm going to graduate, you know."

She sat down and showed him how to find the secret place on his own. It took him a couple of tries, but soon I heard a rip. "I did it! I opened the string cheese!" Nick exclaimed.

He was as happy as a writer whose ink is flowing again.

Ten

Thou Shalt Not Covet Thy Neighbor's Prose*
*or, how to write in a voice all your own

DO YOU LIKE PARLOR GAMES? One of my favorites is called Impostor. It combines two excellent activities, acting and writing. The game is played with three or more players, a room full of books, pencil and paper, and a flair for mimicry. In each round a new leader plucks a book from the shelf, announces its title and author, and reads the first paragraph out loud. The players then write down a phony last sentence of the book on a scrap of paper, trying to mimic the author's style. The game master writes the real last sentence on his own scrap. Then he reads them all to the group—the authentic last line along with the impostors. Finally the players vote on which ending they think is the real one. You earn one point for guessing the true last line and one for each player whom you fooled.

Impostor is a terrific game for readers and writers. But if played too often, it carries a high risk of an infectious disease known as Literary Laryngitis. This lethal illness begins by attacking your idea drive and then spreads to your stylistica oblongata, a region in the brain responsible for one's writing style. If left untreated, it can kill your originality. You end up a witless clone of the writers you were trying to impersonate, and just when you are starting to develop a voice of your own, that voice is lost.

Some people play Impostor without even knowing it. I was one of those unconscious contestants in tenth grade, when I developed a severe case of Literary Laryngitis. I had just finished reading *The Great Gatsby* twice in a row. The moment I closed the book, I felt a passion to write like—no, to *be*—F. Scott Fitzgerald. I would copy pages from his novel into my journal, sleep with his book under my pillow, and eat with it beside my plate.

"George," I said to my high school English teacher one day (he didn't mind if we called him by his first name), "I'd like to read *Tender Is the Night* for my next book report."

"Didn't you just read *The Last Tycoon*?" he asked.

"Yes. And *The Collected Stories* before that. I'm going to read every word Fitzgerald ever wrote."

"*Only* the words he wrote?"

"Don't worry," I said, "he's written tons."

My Fitzgerald obsession was like a movie star or rock star obsession that you may have gone through. You know how at times there are one or two actors or singers whom you just can't get out of your head? You see all their movies or buy all their CDs, clip the articles about them in *People* magazine, and write fan mail that never gets a response. You become so obsessed with your movie or music idols that you start dressing like them, walking like them, talking like them.

I had just this sort of crush on F. Scott Fitzgerald. I didn't just admire the writer; I coveted his prose.

That semester we had to write a short story. I wrote mine in glowing, gooey, grotesque imitation of Fitzgerald. I still remember the last sentence: *So we trudge on, nerds against the grain, groping our uncool way toward the distant light ahead.*

Awful, isn't it? I got it back with a D for "do it over," along with an order that I forfeit all my F. Scott Fitzgerald books for safekeeping—"until you get your voice back."

The next day I hauled a tower of books to class and handed them over to George. He had notified the librarian that the letter *F* was off limits to me. If I wanted to read William Faulkner or Ford Madox Ford, she would send an aide to get their books for me. I went through a miserable week of F. Scott withdrawal, followed by a deep depression and crisis of self. Who was I, if not a character as smooth and sophisticated as Nick Carraway? How could I speak, if not in the voice of Armory Blaine? Under the harsh restraining order to keep away from my idol, how would I ever touch a pen again?

The next semester I read W. Somerset Maugham, Jules Verne, Charles Dickens, Jonathan Swift, Leo Tolstoy, and Richard Wright. I plunged into *The Grapes of Wrath, The Stranger, To Kill a Mockingbird,* and *Lord of the Flies.* A librarian's aide brought me Faulkner's *The Sound and the Fury,* and I read it twice—once to fall in love with it, a second time to understand why. Before long the sound of Fitzgerald's style faded from my ear, his vocabulary let go of mine, and my own sentences uncurled themselves into the straight path that was authentically me.

It's wonderful to admire others, but don't be an impostor—

if you speak too much in someone else's voice, you'll forget how to use your own.

Plagiarism: The Death of Pride

Excessive, self-aggrandizing, big-shotted pride is a sin. Quiet pride, the result of hard work many times revised, is not.

There is a third kind of pride—you could call it poor man's pride—in which someone gloats over work he has copied, downloaded, purchased, or out-and-out stolen but passed off as his own. This is the false pride of plagiarism, and believe it or not, I've seen it displayed before a class of twenty-three unsuspecting students (and one clueless teacher).

His name, for the purpose of this book, was Paul S. His assignment was to write a narrative poem of at least sixteen lines (eight rhyming couplets) about a historical person or event. We had read "Paul Revere's Ride," which I tried to pitch as the first American rap song, and which the students had performed in groups, complete with drum rattles, microphone spitting, and hip-hop strutting around the class. By the time Longfellow had finished with them, they'd been pumped up with Revolutionary fervor and were eager to write and perform narrative poems of their own.

"'Hey, hey, listen up, story's comin' at ya / It's the tale of a queen named Cleopatra,'" one student rapped. "'Only way she could cure a lover's heartache / Was to die by the bite of a poisonous snake.'"

The rhythm had its bumps, a few of the rhymes felt forced, but by the time she had finished her Egyptian rap, her classmates were on their feet, rocking to history.

We had raps about the first moonwalk, the decapitation of Marie Antoinette, the big bang, Noah's ark, and the Los Angeles earthquake of 1994. We even had a somber poem about World War II that ended, "It was a dark and dreary time / Too sad for this or any other rhyme."

When I called Paul up to read his narrative poem, he hesitated for a second and said, "I couldn't think of a historical event, so I just wrote about getting a haircut."

"Well, let's hear it," I said. His classmates chanted his name, and soon he was standing in front of the room, his handwritten poem raised to read. This is how it went:

Once upon time about a week ago
All of a sudden trouble started to grow
My dad said, "Get up, on the double!
Come with me, 'cause you're in deep, deep trouble."
So here's what happened in my tale of sadness
I got dragged down the street by his royal dadness
We rounded the corner and came to a stop
He threw me inside Jack's barber shop
I said, "Please sir just a little off the top."
Dude shaved me bare, gave me a lollipop.
So on my head there's nothing but stubble
I guess I'm stuck in deep, deep trouble.

I was stunned. This back-of-the-room kid, shy by nature, silent by choice, was a gifted poet inside his shell. The class must have been just as surprised; his words, like the hand of Midas, had turned them all to openmouthed statues.

I broke the silence with my applause. Paul's peers began to clap for him too. He stood there, flushed with pride, and then took a smiling bow before returning to his seat.

After Paul's triumphant reading, the bell rang and I dismissed the class. All the students bolted out the door—all but one.

"Mr. Frank."

I looked up and saw Paul's best friend, Daniel, standing across from my desk.

"What is it, Dan?"

"Do you watch *The Simpsons*?"

"Only when I have the time. It's a terrific show, but I'm usually working when it comes on."

"Well, did you know they've got a CD out?"

"No."

"*The Simpsons Sing the Blues*. You should listen to it." Then he paused a moment before saying, "I'm pretty sure Paul has."

Daniel looked at me with troubled eyes. He was telling me something that could hurt his friendship but might help his friend.

On my way home I stopped at the library and listened to *The Simpsons Sing the Blues*. The fifth track began as follows:

Once upon a time about a week ago
All of a sudden trouble started to grow

The next day I asked Paul to stay for a few minutes after school. In the privacy of an empty classroom, I opened my briefcase and handed him the CD, which I'd checked out of the library. Neither one of us spoke. We just stood on either side of the desk staring at each other.

Then Paul's eyes filled with tears. "I couldn't think of anything, Mr. Frank. I didn't know what to write."

"I'm sorry my assignment frustrated you. Maybe you needed more time. Or some help."

He shrugged. "Are you going to give me an F?"

It was a good question. Obviously he deserved an F, but if I gave him one, it would break my record. Like a cop who's never fired his gun, I was a teacher who had never flunked a student.

"I'm going to give you an A," I said.

This was not the punishment he expected.

"But I deserve an F. Why give me an A?"

"Because you're going to do two things to earn it. One—apologize to the class. And two—write a narrative poem of your own, with help if you'd like it."

"What if my narrative poem sucks?"

"You'll still get an A."

For the next twenty minutes Paul and I brainstormed. I discovered that he loved rock 'n' roll and wanted to write about the Beatles. He had an idea for an opening but wasn't sure where to go from there. His first two lines were, "Listen my classmates, I'm gonna tell / About a Liverpool group that you know well." Using the chalkboard as our scratch pad, we jotted down the names of the four Beatles and started to make a make a rhyming tree out of them. Then I asked Paul to think of words or catch phrases that he associated with the band or their songs and make a rhyming tree out of those too. After a while, the chalkboard looked something like this:

John	*Ringo*	*George*	*Paul*
Fabulous	Help me if	read the news	above
Four	you can	today oh boy	song/wrong
I wanna hold	Ed Sullivan	poem home	John gone
your hand	Show	All you need	
John gunned	band	is love	
down			

An hour later several pages of a yellow pad were filled with Paul's jagged handwriting. He said he would type up the poem for the next day, and then he thanked me for showing him how to get started.

On his way out, he paused and turned back.

"Mr. Frank?"

"Yes, Paul?"

"How did you know about the CD?"

"Oh, that. Well . . ."

There are many benefits to being married. Companionship, a second income, and daily advice on what to wear are just a few. But perhaps the best wedding gift you'll ever receive is the life-long white lie you can use whenever the truth is simply unspeakable. I couldn't tell Paul that his best friend had tattled on him, even though I knew that instance of tattling to be an act of compassion. So I told a white lie.

"My wife."

"Your wife?"

"She saw your poem on my desk while I was grading papers. She's a big fan of *The Simpsons*."

There was a pause. Then Paul said, "Well, tell her thanks."

The next day I invited Paul to the front of the class. I encouraged him with a nod. And he spoke.

"I have something to say. It's about the poem I read you guys yesterday. The thing is, I didn't write it. I took it from *The Simpsons Sing the Blues*. You guys clapped for me, but I didn't deserve it. And I wanted to say I'm sorry."

The room was silent as Paul pulled a piece of paper from his pocket. "I worked on a new poem. My own poem. Mr. Frank helped me a little, but it's really my work. I promised him I'd read it to you, so here goes."

And *this* is what Paul read to the class:

Fabulous

Listen my classmates, I'm gonna tell
About a Liverpool group that you know well
A famous '60s rock 'n' roll band
They sang us a song about holding your hand
George, Paul, John, and Ringo
They rocked the world on the Sullivan show
We dug their music, we had to have more
Dance songs and love songs from this fabulous four
They said all we needed was love, love, love
This simple message made us soar above
If only they'd followed the words to their song
They might've stayed together, but something went
   wrong
Too much fortune and too much fame
And before they knew it things weren't the same

Each Beatle let go of the other's hand
And that was the end of the Liverpool band
The story gets sadder, I have to go on
To 1980, with the death of John
Gunned down in front of his New York home
The '6os poet had sung his last poem
There was nothing to do but just look around
And sing, "Help me if you can, I'm feeling down."
Something *did* help us to feel less sad—
It was the Beatles albums that we still had.
So remember, my classmates, to take each other's hand
And listen to the message of that Liverpool band.

I will never forget the look of genuine pride on Paul's face as
he stood in front of his classmates, the object of their applause.
Yes, he had had a little help from a teacher, but it was no more
than the gentle prodding of someone more experienced, no different from the kind of push and consultation that George
Schoenman or my older brother or my Auntie Hankie had once
given me.

Plagiarism is a crime: not only against the writer whose
words you pass off as your own, but against yourself. If you
can't think of anything to write, ask for more time and a little
guidance. When your own voice finally does come out, it may
surprise you.

The Year Your Voice Breaks

You can tell when a boy is going through puberty—just listen to
his voice. A girl's voice may not crack in quite the same way, but

hers too starts to change. All teen voices do. They go back and forth between monotone and exuberant, vulnerable and argumentative, silly and serious, arrogant and unsure. They yell insults at parents, whisper secrets to friends, sing the lyrics to favorite songs, and grunt at all things unfair. But by the time you emerge from the dark ages of adolescence, the gravel will have gone out of your voice, and a new confidence will have found its way in.

Your writer's voice is going to crack too. And like the voice in your throat, the voice in your pen will eventually mend—as long as it's given a chance.

One year I taught a gifted seventh grader named Renata. She loved to craft stories for English and then read them aloud to her classmates. Sophisticated, sensitive, and insightful, her writing captured the angst of her age. The students listened to her, looked up to her as an older sister who had peeked around the corner of adolescence and was back with a preview.

The last project of the year was an analysis of a genre. The students read a collection of short stories (science fiction, horror, mystery, adventure, etc.) and then wrote an essay on the features of that genre. For bonus points they could write a short story of their own.

Renata asked if she could analyze *Nine Stories* by J. D. Salinger. I told her I thought he was a wonderful writer—I had read the collection myself in high school—but she might get more out of them if she waited a couple of years.

"That's okay," she said. "My mom's a writer. She thinks I'm ready for them now."

A month later Renata turned in a brilliant paper on *Nine*

Stories. She analyzed Salinger's themes, style, setting, and characterization. Her paragraphs had near-perfect structure, and her analysis was supported by quotes from the stories themselves. I was on the verge of giving her an A followed by a picket fence of plus signs, when I remembered something she had said: *My mom's a writer.*

"Renata, I loved your paper on Salinger," I told her the next day.

"Thanks, Mr. Frank. The stories were really cool."

"And you understood them so well."

"They weren't that hard. And if there was anything I didn't get, I just asked my mom."

"Did she help you with the essay at all?"

"She typed it for me. But I told her what to write."

"Did she type exactly what you said?"

"Mostly. She changed a few things."

It turned out that Renata's mom had put an adult spin on her daughter's sentences, lengthening some and lightening others, seasoning paragraphs with literary terms that she hadn't used since college, which was the level her daughter's essay had attained on her computer.

"How does that feel, when she changes what you write?" I asked Renata when she told me the true extent of her mom's help.

"Well, she does it all the time. I guess I'd like her not to."

"Have you tried talking to her?"

She looked away. "She'll say I'm being defensive. She always says that when I complain about anything." After a moment she looked back at me and said, "Will you talk to her?" And I said I would.

Putting the Internet to one of its most effective uses—a parent-teacher conference—I sent Renata's mother an e-mail asking her to clarify the role she'd played in preparing her daughter's essay. She wrote back that all of the ideas were Renata's but that she'd put a little "window dressing" on the final draft. She then explained that she was a professional writer (a list of her published books followed) and that she had only been trying to help her daughter develop a more sophisticated writing style by reworking some of her sentences.

A perfectly innocent maternal instinct, right?

Wrong.

There's a reason why teenagers scream, "Get out of my room!" at their parents. There's a reason why they slam and lock their door and blast the words to their favorite rock songs. It's the same reason my daughter pushes me away if I try to help her put her shoes on the correct feet.

"I can do it!" she shouts. And even though I know she's doing it wrong, I have to sit back and let her. When we walk down the block, she may be taking lopsided steps, but as long as she doesn't drift into traffic, I have to let her walk her own way. Eventually she'll realize that the right shoe is on the left foot and the left shoe is on the right, and she'll swap them. Or maybe she'll decide that her feet are just going to have to fit the new arrangement, because she likes it that way. The point is, they're her shoes, her feet, her stride.

It was the year Renata's voice broke, and just as she was

struggling to put it back together again, her mother wanted to sing a duet. I clicked on "reply" to her e-mail:

Dear Mrs._____,

Last Thursday, when the lunch bell rang, everyone in your daughter's class sat still. Not a single bladder had to be emptied or a single stomach had to be filled. No pages shuffled. No backpacks zipped. The students were free to go, but they all chose to stay.

Renata's voice filled the room. She was reading a short story she had written in class about a brother and sister who visit their grandparents. Enemies on the train ride there, they are friends on the way home. The sudden death of their grandfather during the visit makes peace between them.

The story is about three pages too long, the dialogue sometimes clunky, and the descriptions in need of a trim. But it's an exquisite story, told in the unedited voice of an adolescent girl—sassy, funny, sad. It's the voice of your daughter.

Read it. Listen to it. It is developing so beautifully, at its own pace and in its own key. Please help it grow on its own. Make comments on her writing, make suggestions, but let Renata hold her own pen.

Sincerely,

Mr. Frank

To Mind or Not to Mind Your E-mails—
That Is the Question

While checking my e-mail recently, I was distracted by the friendly *brrrrinnnggg* of an instant message alert. It came from a screen name I didn't recognize: COYKITTY21.

"Mr. Frank?????????" it read. "It's me, Leslie."

Leslie was a superstar in my English class, as perceptive and sophisticated a writer as I've ever taught.

"Hello, Leslie," I wrote. "Why aren't you doing my homework?"

"i already finished," she shot back. "2 ez 4 me. u shouldve made it harder."

I blinked, mortified. She had decapitated the letter *I,* misspelled *you,* and forgotten the apostrophe in *should've.* What would my employers say if they read a transcript of our chat? "Mr. Frank, your students can't write at all. You're fired!"

The following day Leslie handed in her composition, "A Character I Created." The assignment was to follow the six methods of characterization to invent an oddball character for a story. With trepidation I read her first paragraph:

Once there was an extremely tall elf named Esther the Jester. She stood a full three inches high in her platform shoes, and she wore extra-wide bell bottom jeans with sequins sewn around the cuffs. Esther lived in the top drawer of a jeweler's workshop. Her dining room table was a magnifying glass which caught the crumbs from Mr. Oogle's daily croissant. Mr. Oogle didn't even know she was there, until the day Esther the Jester saved his life.

Thank God! I thought. Here was the authentic A student I knew. The punctuation was in place. Not a single word was misspelled. All the proper nouns stood tall.

I had heard there was a computer virus that steals your screen name and password; the hacker can then go online and instant-message others while impersonating you. He can even send embarrassing e-mails from you to everyone in your address book.

"Leslie," I told my A student as I handed back her portrait of Esther the Jester, "I'm afraid I have some bad news for you."

"You didn't like my characterization?"

"I loved your characterization. I read it with a tremendous sense of relief."

"What's wrong, then?"

"It's about your screen name. CoyKitty21, right?"

"That's right."

"It's been stolen."

Her eyebrows reached toward each other, as though they were trying to hold hands.

"I'm sorry to be the one to tell you, but you'll have to change it. You'd better get yourself a good antivirus program too, because somebody's been using your screen name. Just the other night I got an instant message from a CoyKitty21."

Her eyebrows slid back into their natural shape. "What did it say?"

"That my homework was too easy. But it couldn't have been you."

"Why not? Your homework *is* too easy for me."

"Because you don't spell the word *too* as a numeral. You know that there are four letters in *easy,* not two, and certainly not a *z*. And you would never leave an apostrophe out of a contraction—*shouldve* instead of *should*-apostrophe-*ve!*"

She looked at me, her lips quivering as though trying not to let go of a laugh. "I think I can keep my screen name, Mr. Frank."

"I wouldn't, Leslie. You've worked hard to build a fine reputation. You don't want it trashed by an impostor."

"There is no impostor. It was me."

"You?"

"I sent you the instant message."

"But you—you assaulted the language."

"It's the Internet, Mr. Frank. We get to leave the rules offline. That's part of the fun."

I don't often peer over my wife's shoulder, but that night, while she sat at her computer answering e-mails, I hovered. Her fingers clicked away speedily, happily. Her shoulders even kept the beat, shimmying a little to the *rat-a-tat-tat* of her typing. I watched her sentences appear on screen, and somewhere in the middle of her second paragraph, there it was—a run-on.

"That should be a semicolon," I pointed out.

Her fingers froze. She swiveled around and cocked her head at me. "Are you correcting my e-mail?"

"You need more of a stop there between those two sentences."

"*Mister* Frank," she said. She only calls me that when I'm in trouble. "I am writing an e-mail to my best friend. We were in high school together. In the same English class. She knows I know how to write a sentence. I'm a writer, for God's sake."

"Well, then, use the language the way it was meant to be used."

"No. I don't have to in an e-mail. E-mail's like a candy store where you can eat all you want and there are no calories. It's somewhere between talking and writing. You don't have to wait for the other person to speak. And you don't have to wait for your brain to think about grammar or your finger to hit the shift key. It's a place to vamp, to be chatty without chatting. To be a more casual, more playful you."

She swiveled away and went back to her fandango typing.

I went into my office, shut the door, and brooded.

Am I being a persnickity Mr. Frank for favoring high standards, even in e-mail? Shouldn't there be someplace, in pixels or in print, where we relax the rules of grammar, spelling, and punctuation, where we *deliberately* violate the Pen Commandments?

I can understand the grammatically challenged shorthand of a chatroom, where you are typing as fast as you can to keep the "conversation" going. I appreciate, even admire, some of the linguistic innovations of instant messaging. When your parent shouts, *"Get offline! It's time for bed!"* G2G for "got to go" is a swifter, smarter response than *I have to sign off now because my parents are pounding on my bedroom door.* And when your chat partner wants to acknowledge something funny you've written, the three little strokes *lol*—"laugh out loud"—are no less than strokes of genius.

But there's a distinction worth making between chatrooms or instant messages and e-mail. Chatting and instant messaging are today's equivalent of the CB radio, a way to communicate with strangers and friends without showing your face. E-mail isn't exactly today's equivalent of the written letter. It is more casual than a letter, yet more formal than an instant message. And unless you have voice-recognition software on your computer, it's still an act of writing.

If I were to give my students a homework assignment to write for fifteen minutes a day, they'd probably groan and beg for relief. But when I ask parents how much time their kids spend online, they tell me an hour, sometimes more. If they are e-mailing or even IM-ing their friends, it's safe to say they're spending at least fifteen minutes in the act of writing. So they're doing my homework without even knowing it.

Young people writing for fun—that's a goal I live for. But not all of my students can keep their online and offline styles segregated the way Leslie does. Many allow the decapitated *i* or the scrunched down *u* to creep into their essay writing, their book projects, or their articles for the school newspaper. This presence of *slong,* or online slang, in their offline writing tells me that a standard of perfection *is* worth fighting for, even in e-mail.

For most of us, e-mail has already replaced letter writing. It's on its way to replacing the phone call, too, as a more convenient way to get or stay in touch with someone. Nowadays if you want to inquire about summer internships at a movie studio, you send an e-mail. If you want to contact your congressperson, you save a stamp. And if you read a magazine or newspaper article or book that moves you to contact the author, you can send an e-mail. You can even conduct an interview through e-mail—send six or seven questions, and several days later you'll get a response.

The response you get—the impression you make—may be affected by how carefully you compose those e-mails. You may not present yourself on paper, but you'll still be presenting yourself in writing.

To mind or not to mind your e-mails, that is the question. Decide for yourselves. But remember that every e-mail you send shows up on somebody's screen, a reflection of you.

How to Live Forever

"He" may turn out to be a great-great-granddaughter, one summer afternoon a hundred years from now, going through boxes in an attic—or the man to whom she's sold the house, without remembering to clean out the garage. But an audience will turn up. In fact, you're counting on it. Someone will be reading and you'll be talking. And if you're talking, it means you're alive.

—THOMAS MALLON, on the inevitable reader
of your diary, in *A Book of One's Own*

I never knew my grandfather Shalom. He died six years before I was born and was alive to me in only two places: the silent black-and-white movies of my parents' wedding, and the stories my mother told me about her dad.

The movies are a family treasure. All my life they've been my only animated glimpse of my grandfather. In them he seems to have a lot of nervous energy, a man whose gestures move faster than the camera recording him. His hair is receding, but where it does grow, it grows with gusto, standing up tall and white, like an approaching wave.

My grandfather was a rabbi—"a rabbi without a hat and beard," as he liked to describe himself. He was also the rabbi at my parents' wedding, which was captured on a Super 8 movie camera held by my father's best man. In the movies my father is thirty, relaxed, debonair, and beaming with joy. My mother is twenty-three. She is as striking as a beauty queen, only a beauty queen who didn't even know she had entered the pageant. She stares at the camera wide-eyed and frozen with fear, as though it weren't a camera but a cannon: you almost expect her to put up her hands in surrender.

When the camera points at Grandpa Shalom, you can see that he knows his daughter is nervous. He also knows, as only a father can, how to help her relax. He is so familiar with the wedding ceremony that he doesn't even need the prayer book to recite the ancient words that unite a woman and a man. But at his own daughter's wedding he pretends to forget. Clowning around, he makes an elaborate gesture of thumbing through the prayer book, shaking his crown of white hair, and slapping his forehead before frantically turning more pages. He tries to say the prayer from memory, falters, and then rummages through the book again. Watching his antics in that faded black-and-white film, I can't help but smile; watching them in person, neither can my mother: the frozen stillness of the young bride suddenly thaws, her face is warmed by laughter, and she turns into a true beauty queen—not one who expected to win the pageant, but one who is glad she did.

A year and a half after marrying my parents, my grandfather was dead. He was fifty-eight.

"Shalom had a wonderful sense of humor," my mother used

to tell my brothers and me whenever something would remind her of him, which was often. She told us stories about his incredible patience with the members of his congregation, who believed that the rabbi's living room was part of the synagogue and that they could drop by anytime. She told us about his coffee addiction, a habit I later adopted and still benefit from. And she told us about his love for Israel, a country he was proud of and fought for even though he visited it just once in his life, the year before he died.

One of my favorite Grandpa Shalom stories is about his two trips to Yosemite—both in a single day. He often went away to a motel to write his sermons. One fall a family friend offered him the use of her cabin in Yosemite, and Shalom drove four hundred miles from Long Beach to work on his sermons for Rosh Hashanah and Yom Kippur. He got there, took one look around, jumped back in the car, and drove the same four hundred miles back to Long Beach. When my grandmother, my mom, and my two uncles heard his Nash pull into the driveway, they all ran out to greet him.

"Shalom," Grandma Sylvia said, "what's the matter? You couldn't think of anything to say on Rosh Hashanah?"

"It's not the sermon," he replied. "It's Yosemite."

"What's the matter with Yosemite?"

"It's beautiful."

"So why come back?"

"I can't work there."

They looked at him like he was crazy. "It's so beautiful," he added, "I don't want to be there without you." And he loaded the whole family into the car and took them with him.

When I wrote the preface to *The Pen Commandments,* I wasn't sure how it would end. But last fall, while helping my mother purge thirty years of accumulated papers, books, bills, photographs, receipts, and her sons' report cards, I saw her come across an old spiral notebook with the words TRAVEL DIARY written on the first page. She opened it, and a postcard fell out—of Mount Meron in Israel, the mountain for which my mother was named.

I looked at the postcard for a moment, and then my eye traveled to the notebook. "Shalom kept a travel diary?" I said.

"Of his trip to Europe and Israel. The year before he died."

I watched her as she flipped through its pages, reading a sentence here, a paragraph there. The expression on her face—the face itself—changed. It was as if my sixty-seven-year-old mother seemed for a moment to grow young, to become a woman of twenty-three as she heard her father's voice again for the first time since he died.

She looked up from the pages and blinked away tears. "It makes me so sad that you never got to meet him."

She looked at the travel diary, then at me. "But you can now," she said. And she introduced me to my Grandpa Shalom:

Tuesday, August 8, 1956—Long Beach

Planned to be in bed at 9 P.M. for good rest. But—7:30 Dr. Moscowitz came with 2 dozen rolls of film. Said he will stay a minute or two, but it was 8:00 before he was about to leave. No sooner was he out the door than in walked Lee Wool, Frieda Kreiger, Rose Ruttenberg. Said they saw the light on. Brought tie

& handkerchief & chocolates—not for me, but for my suitcase. Asked me to deliver them to their families in Israel. Said will stay but a minute—8:30 . . . 9 . . . 10 . . . I was growing weaker . . . 10:30 they asked for another cup of tea . . . 11:00 baruch hashem—*ready to leave, another 10 minutes at the door, my bladder full, more good-byes—11:15 in pajamas, peaceful, & just ready to lie down when—the bell—Mrs. K. come to say "bon voyage" & would I mind taking her son a sweater she knitted.*

Like a character in an Isaac Bashevis Singer story, my grandfather, under siege from his congregation, finally makes it to bed. And when he arrives at the airport the next morning, he has to pay an excess baggage fee, as his modest carry-on has grown to the size of a crate.

On the plane he writes an entry from the Sky Lounge, where he marvels at the human accomplishment of flight:

What a strange animal man is, wonderful & extremely wise & extremely stupid—7 hours & 5 minutes to New York, in a machine that soars to 19,000 feet, flying 375 miles per hour, yet feels like we're hardly moving. If man would make progress & not war, how miraculous & abundant life could be.

My grandfather, like my mom, was a people person. Wherever he went, he struck up a conversation, he made a friend. In London he asks a man for directions to the synagogue:

He walked with me, asked how I liked London. Told him I love it. Can't understand why people say that the English are cold and

*aloof. Find them warm & friendly. He: "Can't say I agree with
you. I'm Scotch, you see."*

On my own first trip to Europe, I fell in love with Rome. So
did my grandfather on his:

*Rome delightful. Weather much nicer than in London. Coffee
much stronger too. Italians are passionate, hot-tempered—torrent
of language when angry & gesticulate with hands. In station
when mailed card to Sylvia, saw woman talk on phone, held several packages, then began to talk loud & fast, put packages down
& began gesticulating with hand into phone—amusing.*

For me, the greatest thrill of reading my grandfather's travel
diary was being able to find out whether my mother had been
telling the truth about him all along. When you grow up hear-
ing how funny, smart, dynamic, and silly your dead grandfather
was—and how devoted to his family—at some point you begin
to question the myth and seek the truth about the man.

"Don't you have anything bad to say about Grandpa
Shalom?" I once asked my mom.

"Yes," she answered. "He died too soon."

When he gets to Israel, he writes something that confirms,
for me, that my mother didn't invent the stories she tells about
my grandfather. She just remembers them:

*Seems preposterous that I have been away from my loved ones just
two weeks. Feels like years. See my mistake. Should have insisted
they come along. Reminds me of Yosemite—have same feeling now.*

I wish my grandfather had kept a journal all his life, instead of on a single trip. But I am grateful to have heard his voice so clearly, in the few pages he left behind.

My Favorite Teacher

You have to write a million words before you find your voice as a writer.

—HENRY MILLER

I have been fortunate to have many excellent writing teachers in my life. The first two were my Auntie Hankie and Uncle Irving. Professional writers themselves, they not only demonstrated the art of writing, they inspired me to follow their path. In ninth grade when I wrote an analysis of *Jane Eyre,* my Auntie Hankie sharpened a blue pencil and drew lines through the clutter in my composition. She never imposed her vocabulary or style on me; she merely chiseled away at my excess. I followed her blue line to the heart of what I had written, and it pointed to a style all my own.

I sailed into high school confident of my writing. The first composition I wrote received a B-minus/C-plus. The man who capsized my ego was George Schoenman. He was also the man who helped repair that ego and make it far more seaworthy than it had been.

My brother Michael is among the most gifted writers I know. He isn't even aware that I consider him one of my mentors. I learn from his example, his persistence, and his eloquence. (I don't let him *actively* teach me, because he is the firstborn and

I am the third, and what younger sibling likes to take advice from an older one?)

But my best writing teacher is the one that has grown with me and remained with me since the day we met. This teacher has thickened over time but maintains an infinite capacity to expand. It gives me the freedom to write whatever I want, from the profane to the profound. It knows everything about me and will keep my secrets as long as I keep it under lock and key. It is the only teacher who always gives me an A.

That teacher is my journal. I started keeping it at age fourteen. Like all teenagers, I needed help figuring out the world around me and finding my place in it. I could write things in my journal that I wouldn't dream of saying out loud, in a voice that would have felt tentative in my mouth but seemed comfortable on the page.

Have you ever listened to your voice on a tape recorder? If you're like most people, the sound of your own voice startles, even disgusts you. Do I really sound like that? you wonder. And when someone tells you that's exactly how you do sound, you never want to open your mouth again. Like your voice on a tape recorder, your voice on the page can come as a surprise. It can be just as mortifying as your spoken voice, particularly when you go back and read an old journal entry. I've gone back and read entries from my early twenties and thought, "How could I have possibly been that troubled, that tortured, that lame?" But as I turn the pages—and the years—I hear my voice shedding its awkwardness, gaining confidence, growing up. In this way, your journal is better than a tape recorder: it doesn't just capture your voice; it sets that voice free, allowing it to mature sentence by sentence, paragraph by paragraph, page by page.

My journal was a safe, secret place to respond to the events of my life. When I fell in love, my journal fell with me. When my heart broke, my journal helped it mend. When I went off to college, my journal came along and helped me figure out what I wanted to study. And when I graduated, it helped me find my way to Europe, to South America, and eventually into a classroom, where my career as a teacher began.

Now, whenever I'm curious about what I felt five years ago, or fifteen, or even twenty, I can flip through my journal and see my thoughts and feelings preserved. I can see the trail of my own past clearly marked, if not always clearly understood, yet I don't need the Ghost of Christmas Past or a time machine to take me there. As Virginia Woolf notes in a page from her diary, "The past is beautiful because one never realizes an emotion at the time. It expands later, & thus we don't have complete emotions about the present, only about the past."

If I can leave you with one piece of advice that I live by, then, it would be to start a journal of your own. You learn to write by writing, and there is no better place to write than in a journal. Give yourself the time to write in it once a day, or once a week, or once a month. Use it as a place to warm up your writing brain, the way a pianist does finger warm-ups or a runner stretches his or her legs. Use it to scrawl your way out of writer's block when nothing else seems to work. If you feel like flaunting the rules of grammar and punctuation, let your journal be the place where you violate all the Pen Commandments (except number 7). But this may surprise you: as your journal grows, your writing will grow with it, and you'll make fewer and fewer mistakes without even trying.

Your journal can be a dumping ground for your frustration, a proving ground for your ideas, a playground for your mind. In the privacy of your journal, you have permission to think, write, and be whatever—or whoever—you want. And you have the privilege to record your life even as it unfolds.

Last summer I had an idea to write an essay about old teachers. (Someday I'll be one myself.) I planned to track down some of the influential figures of my days at Wonderland Avenue Elementary School, Bancroft Junior High, and Fairfax High. At the top of my list was George Schoenman, my high school English teacher. I wanted to thank him for all he taught me. And I wanted to hand him a copy of this book I've written, inscribed "to the man who pointed the way."

My search didn't get far before I learned that George had died of leukemia. Tall and thin, with a nose like a boot in confident stride and a head unabashedly bald, he used to conduct his English class as a conversation among intelligent people. He spoke to us—*with* us—about existentialism, economy of language, structure, and of course the Dodgers. He loved Hemingway and seemed like a character out of *The Sun Also Rises,* a man of hidden but deep emotion who feared getting too close to his students because he knew they would leave him behind. We never thought that he'd be the one to leave us behind.

Ever the existentialist, George used to tell us that from the moment we are born, we start to die. He wasn't trying to scare us; he just wanted us to realize that our time here is finite, and that we should live each day as though it were our last.

Chances are, today won't be your last. Chances are, you *will* get old. People will come in and out of your life, just as ideas will come in and out of your head and feelings in and out of your heart. With a journal you can hold on to them. With a journal you can travel back in time. With a journal you can travel *forward* in time and speak to your grandchildren long before they're born and long after you die.

I've been away from my own journal for a few months, and I'm anxious to get back. I know just what I'll write about first. I'm looking at it now, a small square of paper, an image in gray and white, of a tiny person caught in a head-on pose, in a warm and safe place where he—or she—is growing. The eye of the ultrasound has captured this first picture of our next child, at age negative twenty-four weeks. She—or he—has one arm raised and a mouth wide open, already waving, already saying, "Look out, here I come!"

It isn't just for me that I write. I keep a journal to keep myself alive, to lock away a memory or a moment in the only vault I know that is immune to time. I hope my children—the one here, the one on the way, and the ones yet to come—will visit me in that same vault and join me there with written words of their own.

I hope you will too.

THE FIRST PAGE OF YOUR JOURNAL

_____
_____
_____
_____
_____
_____
_____
_____
_____
_____
_____
_____
_____
_____
_____
_____
_____
_____
_____
_____
_____
_____
_____
_____
_____
_____
_____
_____
_____

Recommended Reading

Just as I've outgrown my one-bedroom apartment on North Kings Road, someday you will outgrow *The Pen Commandments*. I hope it will always be a familiar friend and that you'll come back and visit often. But as you and your writing grow more sophisticated, you'll find that you need the wisdom and guidance of an older and wiser guide than Mr. Frank. When that happy time comes, I hope you'll turn to a few of the books on writing that have helped and inspired me:

King, Stephen. *On Writing: A Memoir of the Craft*. New York: Scribner, 2000.

Lamott, Anne. *Bird by Bird: Some Instructions on Writing and Life*. New York: Pantheon Books, 1994.

Strunk, William, Jr. and E. B. White, *The Elements of Style*. Needham Heights, Massachusetts: Allyn & Bacon, 2000.

Ueland, Brenda. *If You Want to Write: A Book About Art, Independence, and Spirit.* St. Paul, Minnesota: Graywolf Press, 1987.

Welty, Eudora. *One Writer's Beginnings.* Cambridge, Massachusetts: Harvard University Press, 1984.

Winokur, Jon, ed. *Advice to Writers: A Compendium of Quotes, Anecdotes, and Writerly Wisdom From a Dazzling Array of Literary Lights.* New York: Pantheon Books, 1999.

Zinsser, William. *On Writing Well: The Classic Guide to Writing Nonfiction.* New York: HarperCollins, 1998.

Appendix: The Top Ten Grammar Mistakes
You Shouldn't Make

MISTAKE	HINT	CORRECTION
1. My parents give an allowance to my brother and I.	When in doubt, kick the other one out.	My parents give an allowance to my brother and me.
	If you kick out "my brother and," you're left with "My parents give an allowance to . . ."	
	The answer is easy to hear: they give an allowance to *me*."	

(continued)

MISTAKE	HINT	CORRECTION
2. Her and me studied for our grammar test together.	When in doubt, kick the other one out. *Her* studied? *Me* studied? Not very hard.	She and I studied for our grammar test together.
3. The dog lost it's bone.	*It's* is a contraction of *it is,* not the possessive form of *it.* The possessive form of *it* is *its.*	It's a shame that the dog lost its bone.
4. Your my best friend.	*Your* is the possessive form of *you.* *You're* is a contraction of *you are.*	You're my best friend. (May I borrow your car?)
5. Everybody does their own thing.	*Everybody* means "every *single* body," so it has to take a singular possessive pronoun (*his* or *her*).	Everybody gets to do his own thing, *or* her own thing, *but not* their thing.

MISTAKE	HINT	CORRECTION
	If you think it's sexist to write *his,* try writing around the situation: *We all get to do our own thing.*	
6. The girls left there purses over their.	*There* is an adverb meaning *not here,* as in "over *there.*" *Their* is the possessive form of *they,* as in "*their* hair."	The girls left their purses over there.
7. Hopefully you'll master these ten basic lessons.	*Hopefully* is an adverb meaning "full of hope." Who is full of hope in the sentence, you or I? You don't master the lessons *hopefully;* you master them *diligently* or *doggedly* or *meticulously.*	I hope you'll master these ten basic lessons.

(continued)

MISTAKE	HINT	CORRECTION
8. Billy felt badly because he got an F on his grammar test.	*Feel,* in the context of how you feel about something, is an emotion verb, not an action verb. (Grammar books call it a linking verb.) It takes an adjective, not an adverb. You feel *happy* today, or *sad,* or *good* or *bad.* But you don't feel *badly* unless someone cuts off your hands.	Billy felt bad because he got an F on his gammar test. He didn't feel well because he got the flu.
	The only exception is your health. When you are healthy, you don't feel *good.* You feel *well.* And when you're sick, you don't feel *bad.* You feel *unwell* (or *lousy* or *mis-*	

MISTAKE	HINT	CORRECTION
	erable). The *good* and *bad* feelings are the emotional ones; the *well* and *unwell* ones are physical.	
9. I'm tired. I'm going to lay down.	*Lay* is the past tense of the verb *lie,* as in "*lie* down." In the present tense, you *lie* down, or out in the sun, or on the couch.	I'm tired. I'm going to lie down.
	Lay also happens to be the present tense of the verb *lay,* as in "*lay* the money on the table." (The past tense of this verb is *laid.*)	
	After the chicken *lay* down for a nap, it got up and *laid* an egg.	

(continued)

MISTAKE	HINT	CORRECTION
10. These rules are so aggravating!	The verb *aggravate* means "to intensify or increase."	These rules are so irritating!
	The verb *irritate* means "to annoy."	
	All these grammar rules might *aggravate* your headache, but if you don't learn them, you will *irritate* your reader.	

Acknowledgments

I am grateful to many people for their help in making this book. To my father, Marty Frank, for his mantra: *patience and perseverance.* To my mother, Merona, who told me wonderful stories when *I* was in the back seat. To Raymond, Esther, and Clara Lisa Kabbaz of the Lycée Français of Los Angeles, who have been kind enough to give me a writer's teaching schedule. To my students, over seven hundred of them, who have taught me how to teach and have often said, "Mr. Frank, you should be a writer." To my high school English teacher, George Schoenman, who lives on in the many minds he taught. And to my brother Dan for his support and humor all my life long.

I am also grateful to my agent, David McCormick of Collins/McCormick; my editor, Edward Kastenmeier at Pantheon Books; and my copyeditor, Janet Biehl.

A separate line of gratitude is in order for one person whose guidance, faith, and editorial prodding transcend our family tie: my brother Michael.

Finally, I would like to thank my loving wife, Julie, whose picture hangs over my desk with the caption: "Your time is up!"